AN ILLUSTRATED GUIDE TO
MODERN
FIGHTERS
AND ATTACK AIRCRAFT

AN ILLUSTRATED GUIDE TO
MODERN
FIGHTERS
AND ATTACK AIRCRAFT

Bill Gunston

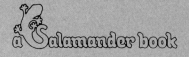

a Salamander book

Published by Arco Publishing, Inc.
NEW YORK

A Salamander Book

Published by
Arco Publishing, Inc.,
219 Park Avenue South,
New York,
N.Y. 10003,
United States of America.

© 1980 by Salamander Books Ltd.,
27 Old Gloucester Street,
London WC1N 3AF,
United Kingdom.

Library of Congress catalog card
number 80-65164

ISBN 0-668-04964-2

All correspondence concerning the
content of this volume should be
addressed to Salamander Books Ltd.

Contents

Aircraft are arranged in alphabetical order of manufacturers' names,
followed by the countries of origin.

Credits

Author: Bill Gunston, former Technical Editor of *Flight International*, Assistant Compiler of *Jane's All the World's Aircraft*, contributor to many Salamander illustrated reference books.

Editor: Ray Bonds
Designer: Lloyd Martin
Three-view drawings:
© Pilot Press Ltd.

Colour profiles: © Pilot Press Ltd., and © Salamander Books Ltd.
Photographs: The publishers wish to thank all the official international governmental archives, aircraft and systems manufacturers and private collections who have supplied photographs for this book.

Printed in Belgium by Henri Proost et Cie.

Aeritalia G91

G91R, G91T, G91PAN and G91Y

Origin: Fiat SpA (now Aeritalia SpA); see text for multinational production of earlier versions.

Type: G91R and Y, single-seat tactical reconnaissance/fighter; G91T, two-seat weapon trainer; G91PAN, single-seat aerobatic display fighter.

Engines: (G91R, T and PAN) one 5,000lb (2268kg) thrust Rolls-Royce (previously Bristol, then Bristol Siddeley) Orpheus 80302 single-shaft turbojet; (G91Y) two General Electric J85-13A single-shaft augmented turbojets each rated at 4,080lb (1850kg) with full afterburner.

Dimensions: Span (G.91R, T, PAN) 28ft 1in (8·57m); (G91Y) 29ft 6½in (9·01m); length (G91R, PAN) 33ft 9¼in (10·31m); (G91T, Y) 38ft 3½in (11·67m); height (G91R, PAN) 13ft 1½in (4m); (G91T, Y) 14ft 6in (4·43m).

Weights: Empty (G91R) typically 7,275lb (3300kg); (G91Y) 8,598lb (3900kg); maximum loaded (G91R) 12,500lb (5695kg); (G91Y) 19,180lb (8700kg).

Performance: Maximum speed (G91R) 675mph (1086km/h); (G91Y) 690mph (1110km/h); initial climb (G91R) 6,000ft (1829m)/min; (G91Y) 17,000ft (5180m)/min; service ceiling (G91R) 43,000ft (13,106m); (G91Y) 41,000ft (12,500m); combat radius at sea level (G91R) 196 miles (315km); (G91Y) 372 miles (600km); ferry range (G91R) 1,150 miles (1850km); (G91Y) 2,175 miles (3500km).

Armament: (G91R/1) four 0·5in Colt-Browning machine guns, each with 300 rounds and underwing racks for ordnance load up to 500lb (227kg); (G91R/3) two 30mm DEFA 552 cannon, each with 125 rounds, and under wing racks for ordnance up to 1,000lb (454kg); (G91Y) two DEFA 552, underwing load up to 4,000lb (1814kg).

History: First flight 9 August 1956; (G91R) December 1958; (G91Y prototype) 27 December 1966; (production G91Y) June 1971.

Users: (G91Y) Italy; (earlier versions) Angola, W Germany, Italy, Portugal.

Development: In December 1953 the North Atlantic Treaty Organisation (NATO) announced a specification for a light tactical strike fighter. It was to be robust, simple to maintain and capable of operation from rough advanced airstrips, yet had to reach Mach 0·92 and be able to deliver con-

Right: Aeritalia G91R/3 of West German Luftwaffe LeKG 43 based at Oldenburg, a light attack unit now receiving Alpha Jets.

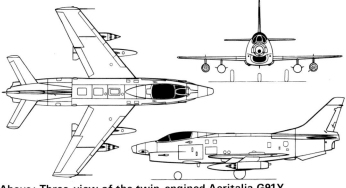

Above: Three-view of the twin-engined Aeritalia G91Y.

ventional or tactical nuclear weapons. There were three French contenders and the G91 from Italy. On the first flight the test pilot lost control and had to eject, but orders had already been placed by the Italian government and production was put in hand. As the design had been based on that of the F-86, but on a smaller scale, the tail problem of the first prototype was soon rectified; but the French refused to have anything to do with the G91 and the original customers — intended to be all the Continental NATO nations — were only Germany and Italy. Italy took 98 G91R/1, 1A and 1B plus 76 G91T/1, while Germany chose 50 R/3, 44 T/3 and 50 R/4, also building a further 294 R/3 under licence by Messerschmitt (later MBB), Heinkel (later VFW-Fokker) and Dornier. The Orpheus was built by a further European consortium. Among many other sub-variants is the PAN version of the Pattuglia Acrobatica Nazionali. The completely redesigned G91Y has much greater thrust, better navigation aids and can fly fighter, attack or reconnaissance missions. Aeritalia, the company formed in 1969 jointly by Fiat and Finmeccanica-IRI, delivered 45 to the Regia Aeronautica in 1971–76.

Below: A fast run at very low level by an Aeritalia G91Y, the twin-engined version now serving with the Italian 8° and 32° wings.

Aermacchi M.B. 326 and 339

M.B.326 and 326 GB and GC (AT-26 Xavante), 326K (Atlas Impala), 326L and M.B.339

Origin: Aeronautica Macchi SpA (Aermacchi); licence-production in Australia, Brazil and S Africa.

Type: Two-seat basic trainer and light attack aircraft; (326K) single-seat trainer/attack; (339) two-seat all-through trainer.

Engine: One Rolls-Royce Viper single-shaft turbojet; (original production versions) 2,500lb (1134kg) thrust Viper 11; (GB, GC, H and M) 3,410lb (1547kg) Viper 20 Mk 540; (K, L and 339) 4,000lb (1814kg) R-R/Fiat Viper 632-43.

Dimensions: Span (over tip tanks) 35ft 7in (10·85m); length 34ft 11in (10·64m); height 12ft 2½in (3·72m).

Weights: Empty (G trainer) 5,920lb (2685kg); (G attack) 5,640lb (2558kg); (K) 6,240lb (2830kg); maximum loaded (G trainer) 10,090lb (4577kg); (G attack) 11,500lb (5217kg); (K and 339) 12,500lb (5670kg).

Performance: Maximum speed (G clean) 539mph (867km/h); (K clean) 553mph (890km/h); (339) 560mph (901km/h); initial climb (G clean) 6,050ft (1844m)/min; (G attack at max wt) 3,100ft (945m)/min; (K clean and 339) 6,500ft (1980m)/min; service ceiling (G trainer clean) 47,000ft (14,325m); (G attack, max wt) 35,000ft (10,700m); range on internal fuel (G trainer) 1,150 miles (1850km); (K with max weapons) about 160 miles (260km).

Armament: Six underwing pylons for load of up to 4,000lb (1814kg) including bombs, rockets, tanks, missiles, reconnaissance pods or gun pods; some versions have single 7·62mm or similar gun (or Minigun) in fuselage; 326K (Impala) has two 30mm DEFA 553 cannon in fuselage, each with 125 rounds. (339) two 30mm DEFA cannon can be carried in wing-mounted slipper pods; other options as 326.

History: First flight 10 December 1957; (production 326) 5 October 1960; (K prototype) 22 August 1970; (339) 12 August 1976.

Users: Argentina, Australia, Bolivia (X), Brazil (X), Dubai, Ghana, Italy, S Africa, Togo (X), Tunisia, Zaire, Zambia, Zimbabwe-Rhodesia (Atlas).

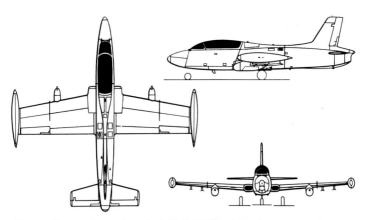

Above: Three-view of typical M.B.326G with wing gun pods.

Development: The most successful Italian military aircraft programme in history, the 326 was designed by a team led by Ermanno Bazzocchi and was put into production as a trainer for the Regia Aeronautica, which received 90. In addition the South African AF has over 150 K models, built by Atlas Aircraft with locally built engines, and expects to build over 200, while other big customers include Australia (114, 85 built by CAC in Melbourne), Brazil (122 locally built Xavantes) and many emergent nations. The latest sub-types are the 326K with the most powerful Viper, the 326L with two seats but K attack capability, the M uncompromised dual trainer and the M.B. 339 with redesigned airframe for all-through training, with raised instructor seat under a sloping canopy. Despite having a largely redesigned structure the 339 is hoped (optimistically) to be priced at only £850,000.

Below left: A formation of South African Air Force equipment, a Mirage IIICZ and DZ with an Impala in the foreground.

Below: By 1980 more than 160 AT-26 Xavantes had been assembled in Brazil by EMBRAER, with American avionics and extra weapons.

BAC (BAe) Lightning

Lightning F.1 to 6 and export versions (data for F.6)

Origin: English Electric Aviation (now British Aerospace), UK.

Type: Single-seat all-weather interceptor.

Engines: Two 15,680lb (7112kg) thrust Rolls-Royce Avon 302 augmented turbojets.

Dimensions: span 34ft 10in (10·6m); length 53ft 3in (16·25m); height 19ft 7in (5·95m).

Weights: Empty about 28,000lb (12,700kg); loaded 50,000lb (22,680kg).

Performance: Maximum speed 1,500mph (2415km/h) at 40,000ft (12,200m); initial, climb 50,000ft (15,240m)/min; service ceiling over 60,000ft (18,290m); range without overwing tanks 800 miles (1290km).

Armament: Interchangeable packs for two all-attitude Red Top or stern-chase Firestreak guided missiles; option of two 30mm Aden cannon in forward part of belly tank; export versions up to 6,000lb (2722kg) bombs or other offensive stores above and below wings.

History: First flight (P.1B) 4 April 1957; (first production F.1) 30 October 1959; (first F.6) 17 April 1964.

Users: Kuwait, Saudi Arabia, UK.

Development: As he had been with the Canberra, "Teddy" Petter was again moving spirit behind the award, in 1947, of a study contract for a supersonic research aircraft. Later this was built and flown as the P.1 of August 1954, exceeding Mach 1 on two crude unaugmented Sapphire engines mounted one above and behind the other and fed by a plain nose inlet. In mid-1949 specification F.23/49 was issued for a supersonic fighter, and after complete redesign the P.1B was produced and flown in 1957. This had a new fuselage with a two-shock intake, the central cone being intended to house Ferranti Airpass radar. The Avon engines were fitted with primitive after-burning, allowing a speed of Mach 2 to be attained on 25 November 1958. Helped by 20 pre-production aircraft, the Lightning F.1 was cleared for service in 1960. Though relatively complicated, so that the flying rate and maintenance burden were terrible in comparison with more modern aircraft, these supersonic all-weather interceptors at last gave the RAF a modern fighter with radar, guided missiles (heat-homing Firestreaks) and supersonic performance. Production was held back by the belief that all manned fighters

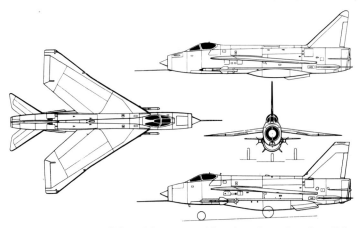

Above: Lightning F.6, with upper side elevation showing F.1.

were obsolete (as clearly set forth in the Defence White Paper of April 1957), but the Treasury were persuaded to allow the improved F.2 to be built in 1961 with fully variable afterburner and all-weather navigation. Eventually, as the error of the 1957 doctrine became apparent, the Mk 3 was allowed in 1964, with more powerful engines, more fuel, bigger fin, collision-course fire-control and allattitude Red Top missiles; but it was decided to fit no guns, earlier marks having had two 30mm Aden cannon. Finally, in 1965, the belated decision was taken to follow the advice of BAC and almost double the fuel capacity and also fit the kinked and cambered wing (first flown in 1956) to improve operation at much increased weights. The T.4 and T.5 are dual conversion trainers equivalent to the F.2 and F.3. For Saudi Arabia and Kuwait, BAC paid for development of the Lightning as a multi-role fighter and attack aircraft, adding 57 to the production total to bring it up to 338.

Left: One of the Lightning F.2A interceptors of 92 Sqn, RAF Germany (a unit since re-equipped with Phantoms) in the one-colour green applied over all upper surfaces to render them less conspicuous when viewed from above.

Below: This Lightning is an F.6, the final standard to which the F.2A (a complete rebuild of a much earlier type) was a near approximation. It is shown unpainted serving with 23 Sqn, and was photographed whilst formating on a Soviet 'Bear' reconnaissance and electronic-warfare aircraft. Today No 23 also flies Phantoms.

BAC (BAe) Strikemaster and 145

BAC 145 and Strikemaster

Origin: Hunting/BAC (now British Aerospace), UK.
Type: Two-seat light tactical aircraft and trainer.
Engine: 3,410lb (1547kg) thrust Rolls-Royce Viper 535 turbojet.
Dimensions: Span 36ft 10in (11·23m); length 33ft 8½in (10·27m); height 10ft 11½in (3·34m).
Weights: Empty 6,270lb (2840kg); loaded (clean) 9,200lb (4170kg); maximum 11,500lb (5210kg).
Performance: Maximum speed 481mph (774km/h); maximum speed at sea level 450mph (726km/h); initial climb (max fuel, clean) 5,250ft (1600m)/min; service ceiling 44,000ft (13,410m); ferry range 1,615 miles (2600km); combat radius with 3,300lb weapon load 145 miles (233km).
Armament: Two 7·62mm FN machine guns fixed firing forwards with 550 rounds each; wide range of stores to maximum of 3,000lb (1360kg) on four underwing strongpoints.
History: First flight (Jet Provost) 16 June 1954; (Strikemaster) 26 October 1967; first delivery 1968.
Users: (Jet Provost) Iraq, Kuwait, Rhodesia, S Yemen, Sri Lanka, Sudan, UK, Venezuela; (Strikemaster) Ecuador, Kenya, Kuwait, New Zealand, Oman, Saudi Arabia, Singapore, Sudan, S Yemen.

Development: The Percival Provost basic trainer flew in February 1950. Hunting then produced a jet version, and flew this in June 1954. Subsequently the Hunting (later BAC) Jet Provost became a successful basic trainer made in great numbers for the RAF and many overseas countries, and more powerful pressurised versions are still one of BAC's current products. From this was developed the BAC.145 multi-role trainer/attack aircraft, which in turn was developed into the highly refined Strikemaster. With a

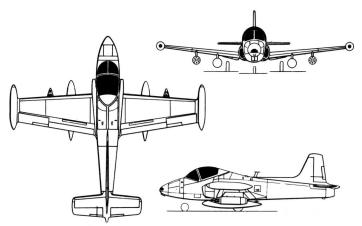

Above: Three-view of basic BAC 167 Strikemaster with rocket pods and tanks.

more powerful Viper engine, the Strikemaster proved to be a great world-wide success. It has side-by-side ejection seats, and the ability to operate from the roughest airstrip whilst carrying a combat load three times a typical bomber's load in the 1930s and any desired equipment fit. The Strikemaster has set a world record for the number of repeat orders placed by its export customers. In early 1977 there were no plans to install the most powerful Viper, the Mk 632, because this would reduce time between overhauls and increase cost without meeting any requirement expressed by a customer. In 1973-76 BAC refurbished 177 RAF Jet Provosts, in the course of which VOR, DME and ILS were installed.

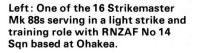

Left: One of the 16 Strikemaster Mk 88s serving in a light strike and training role with RNZAF No 14 Sqn based at Ohakea.

Below left: Kuwait is one of the several states whose Strikemasters – in this case designated Mk 83 – have seen real action.

Below: Another air force whose Strikemasters have been fully used is the Sultan of Oman's; note bomb and Sura rockets on this Mk 82.

Cessna A-37 Dragonfly

A-37, -37A and -37B (Model 318E) (data for -37B)

Origin: Cessna Aircraft Co, USA.

Type: Two-seat light strike aircraft.

Engines: Two 2,850lb (1293kg) thrust General Electric J85-17A single-shaft turbojets.

Dimensions: Span (over tip tanks) 35ft 10½in (10·93m); length (not including refuelling probe) 29ft 3in (8·92m); height 8ft 10½in (2·7m).

Weights: Empty 6,211lb (2817kg); loaded 14,000lb (6350kg).

Performance: Maximum speed 507mph (816km/h) at 16,000ft (4875m); initial climb at gross weight 6,990ft (2130m)/min; service ceiling 41,765ft (12,730m); range (maximum weapons) 460 miles (740km), (maximum fuel) 1,012 miles (1628km).

Armament: One 7·62mm GAU-2B/A six-barrel Minigun in nose; eight wing pylon stations, two inners for up to 870lb (394kg), intermediate for 600lb (272kg) and outers for 500lb (227kg); maximum ordnance load 5,680lb (2576kg).

History: First flight (XT-37) 12 October 1954; (YAT-37D) 22 October 1963; (A-37B) September 1967.

Users: (T-37) Brazil, Burma, Cambodia, Chile, Colombia, W Germany, Greece, Jordan, Pakistan, Peru, Portugal, Thailand, Turkey, US Air Force, Vietnam; (A-37) Brazil, Chile, Ecuador, Ethiopia (delivery embargoed at time of writing), Guatemala, Honduras, Peru, Uruguay, US Air Force and National Guard, Vietnam (left by US forces).

Development: The Cessna Model 318 was the first American jet trainer. It entered production for the US Air Force as the T-37A, powered by two 920lb (417kg) thrust Continental J69 (licence-built Turboméca Marboré) engines and with side-by-side ejection seats. All A models were subse-

Below: The A-37B Dragonfly has been sold to numerous air forces, especially those of South America. These are aircraft of (left) the Fuerza Aérea Ecuatoriana, (upper right) the Fuerza Aérea de Chile and (lower right) the Fuerza Aérea Uruguayana.

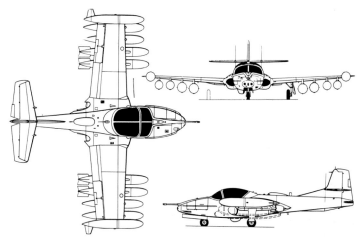

Three-view of A-37B Dragonfly, showing the almost grotesque array of possible stores.

quently converted to the standard of the main production type, the T-37B, with J69-25 engines of 1,025lb (465kg) thrust. Export versions were designated T-37C, with provision for underwing armament. Production of the T-37 was completed in 1975 with more than 1,300 delivered to the USAF and 14 other air forces. It was logical to fit the much more powerful J85 engine and restress the airframe to carry greater loads in arduous combat duties. The work began in 1960 at the time of the upsurge of interest in Co-In (counter-insurgency) aircraft to fight "brushfire wars". Deliveries of A-37A aircraft converted from T-37 trainers began in May 1967 and a squadron of 25 had flown 10,000 combat missions in Vietnam in an extensive evaluation by early 1968. The slightly more powerful A-37B is the definitive production version and by 1977 deliveries had exceeded 600. The A-37B is not pressurised, nor does it have ejection seats, but the dual pilots are protected by layered nylon flak curtains. The wealth of nav/com avionics and possible underwing stores is impressive and nearly all B models have a fixed nose refuelling probe.

Above: Yet another of the Latin American air arms to rely on the warlike Cessna is the Fuerza Aérea del Peru. A total of 36 are in service, all flown by Grupos 13 and 21 from the major FAP base at Chiclayo. Peru's difficulties in procuring later attack aircraft from Western sources caused it to select the Sukhoi Su-22, which when delivered lacked adequate nav/attack avionics.

Dassault Mirage F1

Mirage F1.C

Origin: Avions Marcel Dassault/Breguet Aviation, France, in partnership with Aérospatiale, with Fairey and SABCA, Belgium, and CASA, Spain; licence production in S Africa managed by Armaments Development and Production Corporation.

Type: Single-seat multimission fighter.

Engine: (F1.C) 15,873lb (7200kg) thrust (maximum afterburner) SNECMA Atar 9K-50 single-shaft augmented turbojet; (F1.E) 18,740lb (8500kg) thrust (maximum afterburner) SNECMA M53-02 single-shaft augmented by-pass turbojet.

Dimensions: Span 27ft 6¾in (8·4m); length (F1.C) 49ft 2½in (15m); (F1.E) 50ft 11in (15.53m); height (F1.C) 14ft 9in (4·5m); (F1.E) 14ft 10½in (4.56m).

Weights: Empty (F1.C) 16,314lb (7400kg); (F1.E) 17,857lb (8100kg); loaded (clean) (F1.C) 24,030lb (10,900kg); (F1.E) 25,450lb (11,540kg); (maximum) (F1.C) 32,850lb (14,900kg); (F1.E) 33,510lb (15,200kg).

Performance: Maximum speed (clean, both versions) 915mph (1472km/h) (Mach 1·2) at sea level, 1,450mph (2335km/h) (Mach 2·2) at altitude (with modification to cockpit transparency and airframe leading edges F1.E capable of 2·5); rate of climb (sustained to Mach 2 at 33,000ft) (F1.C) 41,930–47,835ft (12,780–14,580m)/min; (F1.E) above 59,000ft (18,000m)/min; service ceiling (F1.C) 65,600ft (20,000m); (F1.E) 69,750ft (21,250m); range with maximum weapons (hi-lo-hi) (F1.C) 560 miles (900km); (F1.E) 621 miles (1000km); ferry range (F1.C) 2,050 miles (3300km); (F1.E) 2,340 miles (3765km).

Armament: (Both versions), two 30mm DEFA 5-53 cannon, each with 135 rounds; five Alkan universal stores pylons, rated at 4,500lb (2000kg) on centreline, 2,800lb (1350kg) inners and 1,100lb (500kg) outers; launch rails on tips rated at 280lb (120kg) for air-to-air missiles; total weapon load 8,820lb (4000kg). Typical air combat weapons, two Matra 550 Magic or Sidewinder on tips for close combat, one/two Matra 530 with infrared or radar homing, and one/two Matra Super 530 for long-range homing with large changes in height. Wide range of weapons for surface attack, plus optional reconnaissance pod containing cameras, SAT Cyclope infrared linescan and EMI side-looking radar.

History: First flight (F1-01) 23 December 1966; (pre-production F1-02) 20 March 1969; (production F1.C) 15 February 1973; (F1-M53, prototype for proposed F1.E) 22 December 1974; (F1.B trainer) 26 May 1976; service delivery (F1.C) 14 March 1973.

Below: Though it has a much smaller wing than delta Mirages this F1.C of the 5ᵉ Escadre de Chasse carries more and lands slower.

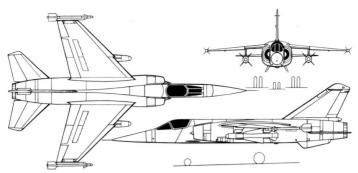

Three-view of the F1.C with Matra R 530s and Sidewinders.

Users: Ecuador, Egypt, France, Greece, Iraq, Kuwait, Libya, Morocco, S Africa, Spain.

Development: Recognising that the Mirage III family would eventually have to be replaced, the French government awarded Dassault a development contract for a successor in February 1964. This aircraft was the large Mirage F2, in the 20 ton (clean) class and powered by a TF306 turbofan engine. It broke away from the classic Mirage form in having a high-mounted conventional swept wing with efficient high-lift slats and flaps, used in conjunction with a slab tailplane. It flew on 12 June 1966. Dassault, however, had privately financed a smaller version of the F2, called F1, sized to be powered by a single Atar engine. This became increasingly attractive and effort was progressively transferred to it from the F2. It went supersonic on its fourth flight and, though it later crashed, the Armée de l'Air decided to buy 100 as replacements for the original Mirage IIIC interceptor and Vautour IIN. Thus was launched an aircraft which in most ways marks a tremendous advance on the tailless delta.

Thanks to the far higher efficiency of the new wing the field lengths and take-off and landing speeds are lower than for the delta Mirages, even though the weights are greater and the wing area much less. Increased thrust comes from the latest Atar engine and among the many less obvious advances are the Cyrano IV multi-mode radar and integral tankage for 45 per cent more fuel (trebling patrol endurance and doubling ground-attack mission radii). Combat manoeuvrability in many situations was increased by as much as 80 per cent and the all-round performance of the new fighter was outstanding. Sales to Israel were prohibited, but orders were soon placed by South Africa and Spain, the former also buying a manufacturing licence. More recently the F1 was chosen by several Middle East countries and many more sales seem certain.

In 1967 the French engine company, SNECMA, began the design of a completely new engine for the Super Mirage. To test the engine the F1 was an obvious choice, and the combination could not fail to be of interest in its own right. The M53 engine confers benefits in acceleration, climb, manoeuvrability and range and, to make up a more modern package, Dassault-Breguet proposed the fully modular Cyrano IV-100 radar and the SAGEM-Kearfott SKN 2603 inertial navigation system, as well as the SFENA 505 digital autopilot of the F1.C. The result is the F1.E, which from early 1974 was strongly, but unsuccessfully, pressed on overseas customers, particularly Belgium, the Netherlands, Denmark and Norway (which agreed a common objective in replacing their F-104Gs). The Armée de l'Air did not want the F1.E, but had agreed to buy a limited quantity had it been chosen by the four NATO nations. Two M53-powered prototypes were flown, but the M53-engined version was shelved in 1975. Today four versions are in production: (C) the basic aircraft, so far chosen by all customers; (E) the C with more advanced avionics (no longer offered with the M53 engine), chosen by Libya; (A) simplified avionics for low-level attack, for Libya and South Africa; (B) two-seater, for Kuwait and Libya.

Dassault
Mirage III and 5

Mirage III and 5

Origin: Avions Marcel Dassault/Breguet Aviation, France (actual manufacture dispersed through European industry and certain models assembled in Belgium, Switzerland and Australia).

Type: Single-seat or two-seat interceptor, tactical strike, trainer or reconnaissance aircraft (depending on sub-type).

Engine: (IIIC) 13,225lb (6000kg) thrust (maximum afterburner) SNECMA Atar 9B single-shaft turbojet; (most other III and some 5) 13,670lb (6200kg) Atar 9C; (some III and 50) 15,873lb (7200kg) Atar 9K-50; (Kfir see separate entry).

Dimensions: Span 27ft (8·22m); length (IIIC) 50ft 10¼in (15·5m); (IIIB) 50ft 6¼in (15·4m), (5) 51ft (15·55m); height 13ft 11½in (4·25m).

Weights: Empty (IIIC) 13,570lb (6156kg); (IIIE) 15,540lb (7050kg); (IIIR) 14,550lb (6600kg); (IIIB) 13,820lb (6270kg); (5) 14,550lb (6600kg); loaded (IIIC) 19,700lb (8936kg); (IIIE, IIIR, 5) 29,760lb (13,500kg), (IIIB) 26,455lb (12,000kg).

Performance: Maximum speed (all models, clean) 863mph (1390km/h) (Mach 1·14) at sea level, 1,460mph (2350km/h) (Mach 2·2) at altitude; initial climb, over 16,400ft (5000m)/min (time to 36,090ft 11,000m, 3 min); service ceiling (Mach 1·8) 55,775ft (17,000m); range (clean) at altitude about 1,000 miles (1610km); combat radius in attack mission with bombs and tanks (mix not specified) 745 miles (1200km); ferry range with three external tanks 2,485 miles (4000km).

Armament: Two 30mm DEFA 5-52 cannon, each with 125 rounds (normally fitted to all versions except when IIIC carries rocket-boost pack); three 1,000lb (454kg) external pylons for bombs, missiles or tanks (Mirage 5, seven external pylons with maximum capacity of 9,260lb, 4200kg).

History: First flight (MD.550 Mirage I) 25 June 1955; (prototype Mirage III-001) 17 November 1956; (pre-production Mirage IIIA) 12 May 1958; (production IIIC) 9 October 1960; (IIIE) 5 April 1961; (IIIR) 31 October 1961; (IIIB) 19 July 1962; (Australian-assembled IIIO) 16 November 1963; (Swiss-assembled IIIS) 28 October 1965; (prototype 5) 19 May 1967; (Belgian-assembled 5BA) May 1970.

Users: (III) Abu Dhabi, Argentina, Australia, Brazil, Egypt, France, Israel, Lebanon, Libya, Pakistan, S Africa, Spain, Switzerland, Venezuela; (5) Abu Dhabi, Belgium, Colombia, Egypt, France, Gabon, Libya, Pakistan, Peru, Saudi Arabia, Venezuela, Zaire.

Right: Like the aircraft above this Mirage IIIEP, of No 5 Sqn Pakistan Air Force, saw actual combat (against India).

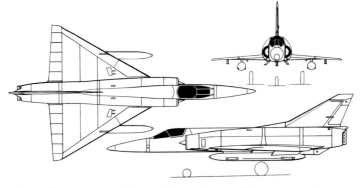

Above: Three-view of Mirage 5, showing multi-sensor pods.

Development: The Mirage, which has come to symbolise modern aerial combat and to bring additional trade to France and incalculable prestige, especially in defence hardware, began in a most uncertain fashion. It was conceived in parallel with the Etendard II to meet the same Armée de l'Air light interceptor specification of 1952 and was likewise to be powered by two small turbojets (but, in this case, boosted by a liquid-propellant rocket engine in addition). As the small French engines were not ready, Dassault fitted the Mirage I with two British Viper turbojets and before the rocket was fitted this small delta was dived to Mach 1·15. With the rocket it reached Mach 1·3 in level flight. But Dassault had no faith in the concept of such low-power aircraft and after some work on the twin-Gabizo Mirage II took the plunge and produced a bigger and heavier Mirage III, powered by the 8,820lb thrust Atar 101G. From this stemmed the pre-production IIIA, with larger but thinner wing and completely redesigned fuselage housing the new Atar 9 engine. On 24 October 1958 Mirage IIIA-01 became the first West European aircraft to attain Mach 2 in level flight.

This clinched the decision of the Armée de l'Air to buy 100 of a slightly developed interceptor called Mirage IIIC, fitted either with guns or with a boost rocket for faster climb and better combat performance at heights up to ►

Left: The fame of the Mirage dated from the amazing air-combat performance of Heyl Ha'Avir pilots in the 1967 war.

82,000ft. Normally the SEP 844 rocket was fitted to the IIIC, the sole armament being air-to-air missiles, such as Sidewinders and the big Matra R.530 used in conjunction with the CSF Cyrano radar, fitted to permit the new fighter to operate in all weather. Altogether 244 C models were delivered, large batches also going to South Africa and Israel (a nation which did much to develop and promote both the III and the 5). From the IIIC emerged the dual-control IIIB trainer, the longer and heavier IIIE for ground attack (with Marconi doppler radar for blind low-level navigation, new fire-control and navigation computer, and increased internal fuel) and the IIIR family of camera-equipped reconnaissance aircraft. By 1977 about 1,200 of the Mirage III family had been sold, including a fairly standard version made in Australia and an extremely non-standard version made in Switzerland after painful development problems which inflated the price and reduced the numbers bought.

In 1965 Israel suggested that Dassault should produce a special VFR (clear weather) version for ground attack in the Middle East, with the radar and fire control avionics removed and replaced by an extra 110 gallons of fuel and more bombs. The result was the Mirage 5 and Israel bought 50 of the first

production batch of 60. It can be distinguished by its longer and much more pointed nose, devoid of radar unless the small Aida II is fitted. For political reasons the French refused to deliver the paid-for Mirages to Israel but more than 500 have been sold to many other countries and 106 were assembled, and partly constructed, in Belgium. Largely as a result of the French action, Israel developed its own improved version of the Mirage (see IAI Kfir, separate entry).

In addition to production aircraft there have been many experimental or unsold variants. One of the latter was the Spey-powered Mirage IIIW jointly proposed by Dassault and Boeing as a rival to the F-5 as a standard simple fighter for America's allies. Another non-starter was the Milan (Kite), fitted with retractable "moustache" foreplanes for shorter field-length and better manoeuvrability (this excellent idea is available on the Mirage 5). By far the biggest development programme concerned the enlarged and more powerful Mirage IIIV V/STOL fighter with a 19,840lb thrust SNECMA TF306 augmented turbofan for propulsion and eight 5,500lb thrust Rolls-Royce RB.162-31 lift jets. The IIIT was a non-VTOL of the same size and the equally large F2 led to the smaller (Atar-size) F1.

Left: Pictured outside the assembly plant near Bordeaux, this Mirage 5DM dual-control trainer was delivered to the air force of Zaire, with two others of this sub-type and 14 single-seaters. Of the total of 17 Mirages no fewer than six were lost in the fighting on the Xhaba battlefront.

Immediately below: The most effective Mirages in the ground-attack role (against enemy radars, at least) are probably the IIIEs of the Armée de l'Air armed with the AS.37 anti-radar Martel. Total production of this extended-range dedicated attack version of the Mirage III was 523.

Foot of page: Nearly all the 27 customers for delta-wing Mirages have bought dual-control trainer versions to accustom pilots to the tricky characteristics of fast-landing deltas which approach 'on the back of the drag curve'. This is a Mirage 5-DV of the Fuerza Aérea Venezolana, whose Mirages are concentrated at the training and attack base of Barquisimento along with CF-5s.

Dassault
Mirage 2000

Mirage 2000 (single- and two-seat versions)

Origin: Avions Marcel Dassault/Breguet Aviation, France.
Type: Multi-role fighter with emphasis on interception and air superiority combat.
Engine: One SNECMA M53-5 single-shaft afterburning by-pass turbojet (low-ratio turbofan) with maximum thrust of 12,350lb (5602kg) dry and 19,840lb (9000kg) with afterburner.
Dimensions: Span 29ft 6in (9·0m); length 50ft 3½in (15·33m).
Weights: Empty, not released; normal takeoff, air-intercept mission 33,000lb (14,969kg).
Performance: Maximum speed at 36,000ft (11,000m) Mach 2·3, 1,518mph (2440km/h).
Armament: Two 30mm DEFA 5-53 cannon; normal air-intercept load two Matra Super 530 and two Matra 550 Magic air-to-air missiles; intention is to develop ground-attack version with maximum overload of 11,025lb (5000kg) of weapons and/or tanks and ECM pods on five external hardpoints.
History: Announcement of project December 1975; first flight 10 March 1978; production delivery, probably late 1982.
Users: Egypt (intended licence-production), France.

Development: In December 1975 the French government cancelled the Dassault-Breguet Super Mirage, which had been publicised as the Avion de Combat Futur and mainstay of the Armée de l'Air in the 1980s. In its place it announced a decision to award a study contract with Marcel Dassault for a smaller and simpler single-engined delta fighter outwardly looking very much like the Mirage III of 20 years earlier. In fact the Mirage 2000 — some-

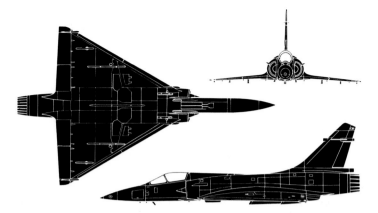

Above: Three-view of Dassault Mirage 2000.

times called the Delta 2000 — will differ significantly from the old Mirage, in aerodynamics, propulsion, structure and equipment. Aerodynamically it will be designed to incorporate American discoveries in CCV (control-configured vehicle) technology, in which aircraft are deliberately made unstable — for example, by positioning the centre of gravity much further back than usual — and using high-authority fail-safe flight-control systems to keep them under control. The result is either a smaller wing or, as in the Mirage 2000, dramatically higher manoeuvrability. Unlike the earlier Mirage deltas the 2000 will have leading-edge devices, either hinged droops or some form of slats, which will work in conjunction with the trailing-edge elevons to counteract the unstable pitching moment, or, in a ▶

Below: The second prototype Dassault Mirage 2000, with two Matra Super 530 air-to-air missiles (which are intended to be a standard weapon on aircraft of this type with the Armée de l'Air).

tight turn, relax their effort or even help the aircraft to pitch nose-up. In the landing configuration the leading-edge devices (the French call it a "variable-camber" wing) will allow the elevons to be deflected down, adding to lift, whereas in earlier tailless deltas they have to be deflected up, effectively adding to weight just at the worst time.

Already the Mirage 2000 is being publicised as "being able to outclass combat aircraft presently being developed and produced in the Western world". It will have: "fly-by-wire" multi-channel electrically signalled flight controls; composite materials, carbon fibre being mentioned; large-radius Karman fairings (a reference to area ruling of the fuselage for minimum transonic drag); an elaborate weapon system with "g.p." (general-purpose?) computer and inertial unit; and long-range digital radar. Ratio of thrust to weight is to exceed unity. Such features are what one would expect of such an aircraft, but the problems are clearly enormous, especially in a time of severe inflation and economic pressures. France has since 1975 made attempts to acquire the base of technology, especially in digital avionics, necessary to build the Mirage 2000, but has little capability as yet. Only a single French aircraft, a two-seat Mirage IIIB with Sfena system, has flown with a primitive fly-by-wire system. Thomson-CSF estimate it will take "seven to eight years" to develop a 170-km-range digital radar needed to match the developed Super 530 missile. France has little experience of advanced composite structures, and that only in small test pieces and helicopters. SNECMA has not announced how the M53 engine, with very limited flight-time and no other application, is going to be increased in thrust by 35 per cent. If the aircraft to fly in 1978 is truly a prototype, and not the first off a production line, it will need everything to go right to meet an in-service date of 1982 with a developed aircraft. Not least, the proposed price of Fr40 to 50 million (£4·5 to 5·5 million) will be extremely difficult to hold, even in December 1975 Francs, because the magnitude of the system-development problems to France appear to have been grossly underestimated.

In the original announcement the Mirage 2000 was described as "limited to high-speed and high-level interception and reconnaissance. . . . Attack and penetration at low levels will be undertaken by a different type." (The cancelled Super Mirage had been intended to fulfil all tactical roles.) But in December 1976 the Chief of Staff of the Armée de l'Air said he personally considered it would be necessary to build an interdictor and reconnaissance (he implied at low level) version of the Mirage 2000. It became known at this time that the new delta will apparently have nine weapon stations, which is diametrically opposed to the uncompromised high-altitude dog-fight concept announced in December 1975; and low-level use is dia-

metrically opposed to a large-area delta. The Armée de l'Air has from the start hoped to buy 200 Mirage 2000s, twice the number it judged it could afford of the Super Mirage. But future progress of the programme, helped by US industry strictly on an inter-company rather than a government basis, will be instructive to watch.

Dassault Super Mirage 4000

Type: Multi-role combat aircraft.
Engines: (prototype) two SNECMA M53-5 single-shaft afterburning by-pass turbojets each with maximum thrust of 19,840lb (9000kg).
Armament: Not fitted to prototype.
History: Company launch January 1976; first flight 9 March 1979.
User: None announced (August 1979).

In January 1976 Marcel Dassault announced that, as a private venture, he was launching the Delta Super Mirage as a long-range multi-role aircraft for export. One hesitates to doubt the credibility of either the man or the company, but to fund such a programme would need many times the net worth of the company, and no consortium of overseas buyers (South Africans? Arabs? Black Africans?) appears to be conceivable. It would not be impossible for the company to finish the defunct tailed Super Mirage prototype, which was to have flown in July 1976, as an empty shell to show possible customers what the proposed Delta Super Mirage would look like. To develop it as an operational aircraft does not by any stretch of the imagination appear possible. One is left to conclude that M Dassault either expects the French government to find the money, which is extremely unlikely, or he hopes to organise a programme involving a large number of nations prepared to share the costs and risks.

Aerodynamically the 4000 closely resembles a scale-up (about ×1·25) of the 2000, but with a proportionately larger fin and the important addition of electrically signalled powered canards on the inlets in place of the smaller fighter's fixed strakes. The radar is the completely new RDM (Radar Doppler Multifonction) Cyrano 500, tested in a Vautour and also intended for export models of Mirage 2000. An I-band track-while-scan set, it is a frequency-agile pulse-Doppler with several functions unavailable in the RDI (Radar Doppler Impulsions) of the regular 2000.

Below: This formation of the Super Mirage 4000 with two prototype Mirage 2000s shows the relative sizes of the two designs, and the slightly different aerodynamics (with controllable foreplanes) of the later twin-engined aircraft.

25

Dassault
Super Etendard

Super Etendard

Origin: Avions Marcel Dassault/Breguet Aviation, France.
Type: Single-seat carrier strike fighter.
Engine: 11,265lb (5110kg) thrust SNECMA Atar 8K-50 single-shaft turbojet.
Dimensions: Span 31ft 5¾in (9·6m); length 46ft 11½in (14·31m); height 12ft 8in (3·85m).
Weights: Empty 13,889lb (6300kg); loaded 25,350lb (11,500kg).
Performance: Maximum speed 745mph (1200km/h) at sea level, Mach 1 at altitude; initial climb 24,600ft (7500m)/min; service ceiling 52,495ft (16,000m); range (clean) at altitude, over 1,243 miles (2000km).
Armament: Two 30mm DEFA cannon; mission load up to 9,921lb (4500kg) carried on five pylons.
History: First flight (converted Etendard) 28 October 1974; first delivery, late 1977.
User: France (Aéronavale).

Development: During the late 1960s it had been expected that the original force of Etendards would be replaced, in about 1971, by a specially developed version of the Jaguar, the M version with single main wheels, full carrier equipment and specially fitted for the naval strike role. A Jaguar M completed flight development and carrier compatability, but for various reasons, mainly concerned with politics and cost, this was rejected by the Aéronavale and a search began for an alternative. After studying the A-4 Skyhawk and A-7 Corsair, the Aéronavale chose Dassault-Breguet's proposal for an improved Etendard. This has a substantially redesigned structure, for operation at higher indicated airspeeds and higher weights; a new and more efficient engine, obtained by removing the afterburner from the Atar 9K-50 of the Mirage F1.C; completely new inertial navigation

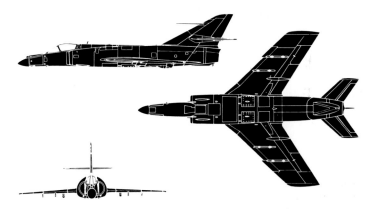

Three-view of the Super Etendard (centreline pylon not shown).

system, produced mainly by SAGEM with American help; new multi-mode nose radar, produced jointly by Thomson-CSF and Electronique Marcel Dassault, with especially good performance in surface vessel detection and attack; and much greater and more varied mission load. Flight development was completed in 1974-77 with three converted Etendard IVs, the first testing the engine, the second the avionics and weapons, and the third the new wing with slats and double-slotted flaps like the Jaguar. In 1973 the Aéronavale announced it would buy 100, but this has now been cut back to 30, and service delivery delayed until late 1978.

Below: Unlike Britain, which has no conventional aircraft carriers, the French Navy has no plans to withdraw either *Foch* or *Clémenceau* from operational commission. Here a Dassault Super Etendard (No 7) is seen aboard the former vessel, though the first dozen aircraft to be delivered went to the land airfield of Landivisiau, where they replaced the obsolescent Etendard IVM. Super Etendards are also replacing Crusader F-8(FN) fighters.

Dassault/Breguet Dornier Alpha Jet

Alpha Jet

Origin: Jointly Dassault/Breguet, France, and Dornier GmbH, W Germany, with assembly at each company.

Type: Two-seat trainer and light strike/reconnaissance aircraft.

Engines: Two 2,976lb (1350kg) thrust SNECMA/Turboméca Larzac 04 two-shaft turbofans.

Dimensions: Span 29ft 11in (9·12m); length (excluding any probe) 40ft 3¾in (12·29m); height 13ft 9in (4·2m).

Weights: Empty 6,944lb (3150kg); loaded (clean) 9,920lb (4500kg), (maximum) 15,432lb (7000kg).

Performance: (clean) maximum speed 576mph (927km/h) at sea level, 560mph (900km/h) (Mach 0·85) at altitude; climb to 39,370ft (12,000m), less than 10 minutes; service ceiling 45,930ft (14,000m); typical mission endurance 2hr 30min; ferry range with two external tanks 1,510 miles (2430km).

Armament: Optional for weapon training or combat missions, detachable belly fairing housing one 30mm DEFA or 27mm Mauser cannon, with 125 rounds, or two 0·50in Brownings, each with 250 rounds; same centreline hardpoint and either one or two under each wing (to maximum of five) can be provided with pylons for maximum external load of 4,850lb (2200kg), made up of tanks, weapons, reconnaissance pod, ECM or other devices.

History: First flight 26 October 1973; first production delivery originally to be early 1976, actually late 1978.

Users: Belgium, Cameroun, France, W Germany, Ivory Coast, Nigeria, Togo.

Development: Realisation that the Jaguar was too capable and costly to be a standard basic trainer led to the Armée de l'Air issuing a requirement for a new trainer in 1967. The chosen design was to be capable of use in the light ground attack role, in which the Luftwaffe had a parallel need for an aircraft. On 22 July 1969 the two governments agreed to a common specifi-

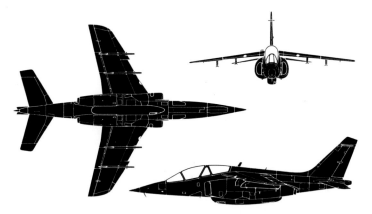

Above: Three-view of Alpha Jet prototype with armament.

cation and to adopt a common type of aircraft produced jointly by the two national industries. After evaluation against the Aérospatiale (Nord)/MBB E650 Eurotrainer, the Alpha Jet was selected on 24 July 1970. Aircraft for the two partners are nearly identical. France makes the fuselage and centre section and Germany the rear fuselage, tail and outer wings. SABCA of Belgium makes minor portions. Engines, originally shared by two French companies (see above), are being produced in partnership with MTU and KHD of Germany, plus a small share by FN of Belgium. Trainer aircraft are assembled at Toulouse (France) and attack versions at Oberpfaffenhofen (Germany). Decision to go ahead with production was reached on 26 March 1975. It was expected at that time that France and Germany would each buy 200, and that Belgium would buy 33, but the programme has slipped by more than two years, resulting in increased costs. In 1979 full production was achieved.

Below: After prolonged delays the Alpha Jet finally got into full service in late 1978, with the specially equipped light attack version for the Luftwaffe following in late 1979.

Fairchild Republic A-10A Thunderbolt II

A-10A

Origin: Fairchild Republic Co, USA.

Type: Single-seat close-air-support aircraft.

Engines: Two 9,275lb (4207kg) thrust General Electric TF34-100 two-shaft turbofans.

Dimensions: Span 57ft 6in (17·53m); length 53ft 4in (16·26m); height 14ft 5½in (4·4m).

Weights: Empty 21,813lb (9894kg); maximum loaded 47,200lb (21,410 kg).

Performance: Maximum speed (clean) 460mph (740km/h), 380mph (612km/h) at maximum weight; initial climb 1,000ft (328m)/min at maximum weight; take-off distance (at maximum weight) 3,850ft (1173m), (at forward-airstrip weight with six Mk 82 bombs), 1,130ft (344m); steady speed in 45° dive with full airbrake 299mph (481km/h); close-air-support radius with reserves 288 miles (463km); ferry range 2,723 miles (4382km).

Armament: 30mm high-velocity GAU-8/A cannon in forward fuselage; 11 pylons for total external ordnance load of 16,000lb (7257kg) (exceptionally, 18,500lb, 8392kg).

History: First flight 10 May 1972; service delivery for inventory December 1974.

User: US Air Force.

Development: Despite the more overt attractions of Mach 2 aircraft the US Air Force was forced to consider the CAS (close air support) mission because of the total unsuitability of its existing equipment. In both the wars it had had to fight since World War II — Korea and Vietnam — its aircraft had been worldbeaters but planned for a totally different kind of war. What was needed, it appeared, was something like an up-to-date Skyraider that could carry a heavy load of ordnance, had good endurance and could survive severe damage from ground fire. Between 1963-69 extensive ▶

Right and below: Thunderbolt IIs pictured during their initial shakedown flying at Davis-Monthan and Nellis AFBs.

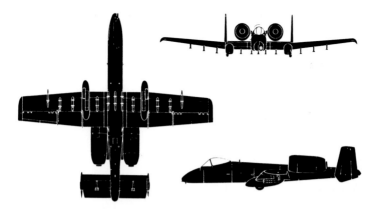

Three-view of standard Fairchild A-10A showing 11 pylons.

studies gradually refined the AX specification, which had begun by pre-supposing a twin turbo prop and ended with a larger aircraft powered by two turbofans. After an industrywide competition the Northrop A-9A and Fairchild A-10A were chosen for prototype fly-off evaluation, which took place with two of each type at Edwards in October–December 1972. The A-10A was announced winner and GE the winner of the contest to produce the 30mm tank-busting gun, the most powerful ever fitted to any aircraft, with very high muzzle velocity and rate of fire, and muzzle horsepower 20 times that of the 75mm gun fitted to some B-25s in World War II. Named Avenger, this gun is driven hydraulically at either 2,100 or 4,200rds/min, and is fed by a drum containing 1,350 milk-bottle-size rounds. Empty cases are fed back into the rear of the drum. By 1978 ground-reloading will probably be done by a special powered system. Underwing load can be made up of any stores in the Tactical Air Command inventory, the landing gears (which protrude when retracted for damage-free emergency landing) and all tail surfaces are interchangeable, the cockpit is encased in a "bath" of thick titanium armour, and the engines are hung above the rear fuselage where their infra-red signature is a minimum. Originally Tactical Air Command intended to buy 600 of these grey-painted brutes, but despite unavoidable escalation in cost and degradation in performance the planned number has grown to 733, of which half had been delivered by 1980 at a current rate of 14 per month.

Above: Thunderbolt IIs on the flight line at Nellis where the USAF Tactical Fighter Weapons Center is located. Operationally the A-10A is classed as a fighter, though this is not its role.

Left: Firing the 30mm GAU-8/A cannon at simulated armour; this is the most powerful gun ever fitted to an aircraft. The pilot has not opened his split ailerons which in dives serve as brakes.

Below: Releasing a Paveway-series Mk 82 laser-guided bomb from level flight. Targets are detected by the Pave passive laser receiver pod seen carried on a pylon under the nose.

FMA IA 58 Pucarà

IA 50 GII, IA 58 and Astafan Trainer

Origin: FMA (Military Aircraft Factory), Argentina.

Type: IA 58, tactical attack and counter-insurgency; IA 50, utility transport and survey; Trainer, trainer and light attack.

Engines: (IA 58) two 1,022ehp Turboméca Astazou XVIG single-shaft turboprops; (IA 50) two 1,000ehp Turboméca Bastan VIC single-shaft turboprops; (Trainer) two 2,710lb (1230kg) thrust Turboméca Astafan geared turbofans.

Dimensions: Span (IA 58 and Trainer) 47ft 6¾in (14·5m); (IA 50) 64ft 3¼in (19·59m); length (IA 50 and Trainer) 46ft 3in (14·1m); (IA 50) 50ft 2½in (15·3m); height (IA 58 and Trainer) 17ft 7in (5·36m); (IA 50) 18ft 5in (5·61m).

Weights: Empty (IA 58) 8,900lb (4037kg); (IA 50) 8,650lb (3924kg); (Trainer) 8,377lb (3800kg); loaded (IA 58) 14,300lb (6486kg); (IA 50) 17,085lb (7750kg); (Trainer) 14,330lb (6500kg).

Performance: Maximum speed (IA 58) 323mph (520km/h); (IA 50) 310mph (500km/h); (Trainer) about 400mph (643km/h); initial climb (IA 58) 3,543ft (1080m)/min; (IA 50) 2,640ft (805m)/min; service ceiling (IA 58) 27,165ft (8280m); (IA 50) 41,000ft (12,500m); range with maximum fuel (IA 58) 1,890 miles (3042km); (IA 50) 1,600 miles (2575km).

Armament: IA 58, and optional for Trainer, two 20mm Hispano cannon and four 7·62mm FN machine guns in forward fuselage; pylons under fuselage and outer wings for up to 3,307lb (1500kg) of stores or tanks.

History: First flight (IA 50) 23 April 1963; (IA 58) 20 August 1969; (service delivery of IA-58) November 1974.

Users: Argentina, Bolivia (?).

Development: The unusual but effective Pucará was derived from the larger IA 50 GII (Guarani II) multi-role transport, noted for its slender unswept wings but sharply swept fin and rudder. The first production batch of GII's comprised 18 to the Argentine Air Force for communications and seating for up to 15 passengers, four as photo survey aircraft with the

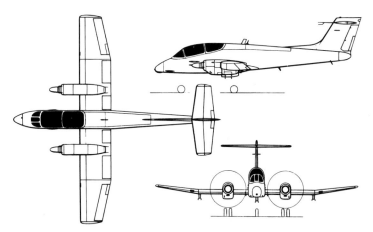

Three-view of IA 58 Pucará in production configuration.

Military Geographic Institute and one as a VIP transport for the President of Argentina. Many others were ordered later, some having ski gear for use in the Antarctic. The smaller IA 58 seats pilot and observer in tandem Martin-Baker ejection seats and is well equipped for all-weather tactical Co-In operations. Deliveries began in 1975 on the first batch of 30 for the Argentine Air Force, with further batches up to a predicted total of 100 being discussed. Interest has been expressed by several other nations in this versatile and cost/effective aircraft, which can operate from rough strips down to about 2,000ft in length. The Trainer uses the IA 58 airframe restressed to have two turbofan engines on the sides of the fuselage, the twin-wheel main gears retracting forwards into wing pods in the same locations as the engine nacelles on the IA 58. It was expected that this project would lead to a tactical Co-In version, but development has been delayed by inflation.

Below: The first production Pucará, which flew in November 1974; about 30 had been delivered by the summer of 1979.

General Dynamics F-16

Model 401, YF-16, F-16A, F-16B

Origin: General Dynamics/Fort Worth, USA, with widespread sub-contract manufacture in Europe and European assembly of aircraft for European customers (see text).

Type: Single-seat fighter bomber; (B) operational trainer.

Engine: One 24,000lb (10,885kg) thrust Pratt & Whitney F100-PW-100 two-shaft afterburning turbofan.

Dimensions: Span (no Sidewinders) 31ft 0in (9·45m), (with Sidewinders) 32ft 10in (10·01m); length (excl probe) (YF-16) 46ft 6in, (F-16A) 47ft 7·7in (14·52m); height (F-16) 16ft 5·2in (5·01m).

Weights: Empty (YF) about 12,000lb (5443kg); (F) about 14,800lb (6733kg); maximum gross (YF) 27,000lb (12,245kg); (F) 33,000lb (14,969kg).

Performance: Maximum speed, Mach 1·95, equivalent to about 1,300mph (2090km/h); initial climb (YF) 40,000ft (12,200m)/min; service ceiling about 60,000ft (18,300m); range on internal fuel in interception mission, about 1,300 miles (2100km); attack radius at low level with maximum weapon load, 120 miles (193km); attack radius with six Mk 82 bombs, 339 miles (546km).

Armament: One 20mm M61 multi-barrel cannon on left side of fuselage; nine pylons for total external load of up to 15,200lb (6895kg) (YF, seven pylons for total of 11,500lb, 5217kg).

History: First flight (YF) 20 January 1974; service delivery, scheduled for mid-1978.

Users: Belgium, Denmark, Israel, the Netherlands, Norway, US Air Force.

Development: One of the most important combat aircraft of the rest of the century was started merely as a technology demonstrator to see to what degree it would be possible to build a useful fighter that was significantly smaller and cheaper than the F-15. The US Air Force Lightweight Fighter (LWF) programme was not intended to lead to a production aircraft but merely to establish what was possible, at what cost. Contracts for two prototypes of each of the two best submissions were awarded in April 1972, the aircraft being the General Dynamics 401 and a simplified Northrop P.530. As the YF-16 and YF-17 these aircraft completed a programme of competitive evaluation, as planned, in 1974. By this time the wish of four European members of NATO — Belgium, Holland, Denmark and Norway — to replace their F-104Gs with an aircraft in this class had spurred a total revision of the LWF programme. In April 1974 it was changed into the Air Combat Fighter (ACF) programme and the Defense Secretary, James ▶

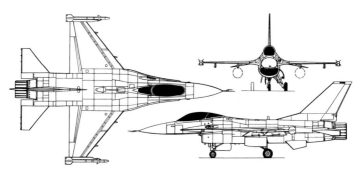

Three-view drawing of production F-16A (nozzle open).

Above: This picture of an F-16 prototype tangling with an RF-4 Phantom emphasizes the contrast in sizes of these classic aircraft, both fighters' which became multi-role platforms. As this book went to press there was no RF-16 dedicated recon type.

Below: One of the eight development F-16s is seen here formating at low speed on a photo aircraft, having to fly at a large nose-up attitude in consequence. The wingtip AIM-9J (to be AIM-9L in production machines) missile is mounted nose-down.

This splendid photograph, taken from the front seat of a TF-104G, shows (left) an F-16A with centreline tank and wingtip AIM-9L Advanced Sidewinder missiles, and (right) a two-seat F-16B with two 308-gal (1400 litre) underwing tanks and AIM-9J missiles on the tips. The photograph was secured in the summer of 1979 during multinational operations with the RNorAF in Norway.

Schlesinger, announced that 650 of the winning design would be bought for the USAF, a number later raised to 1,388. In December 1974 the YF-16 was chosen as the future ACF (announced the following month) and in June 1975, after protracted and tortuous discussions, it was chosen by the four European countries. As an aircraft the F-16 is exciting. It has a flashing performance on the power of the single fully developed engine (the same as the F-15) fed by a simple fixed-geometry inlet. Structure and systems are modern, with control-configured vehicle (CCV) flight dynamics, quad-redundant electrically signalled controls (fly-by-wire), graphite-epoxy structures and a flared wing/body shape. Pilot view is outstanding and he lies back in a reclining Escapac seat and flies the aircraft through a sidestick controller. In the nose is an advanced pulse-doppler radar suitable for attack or interception missions and armament can be carried for both roles, though the basic design was biased strongly in favour of air-to-air missions in good weather at close range. It remains to be seen to what degree the F-16 can be modified to make it a better ground attack, reconnaissance or all-weather interceptor aircraft. Main contractors include Westinghouse (radar), Marconi-Elliott (HUD-sight and portions of flight-control system), Westinghouse and Delco (computers), Kaiser (radar and electro-optical display) and Singer-Kearfott (inertial system). In 1977 the USAF still intends to purchase 650 aircraft, mainly for use in Europe; in 1976 it set up a European System Programme Office to manage the project,

Above: Takeoff of the first Belgian F-16B assembled by SABCA.

Below: A grey-painted development (pre-production) F-16A.

USAF
50748

40

and began work on the support depot. Orders are still subject to change, but the planned totals are: Belgium, 90 F-16A and 12 F-16B, with 14 aircraft on option; Denmark 48 (probably 40+8), and 10 on option; the Netherlands, 84, plus 18 on option; Norway, 72 (no options). In July 1976 General Dynamics finally signed co-production contracts with major companies in Belgium and Holland, specifying schedules and output rates, of parts for 564 aircraft, a total that would increase with further F-16 sales. Aircraft will be assembled by General Dynamics (USAF), Fairey/SABCA (Belgium and Denmark) and Fokker-VFW (Netherlands and Norway); Kongsberg in Norway has a $163m co-production deal with Pratt & Whitney on more than 400 engines (all engines will be assembled by P & WA). Since early 1976 Turkey has been negotiating to join the European consortium (which has no formal title) and to buy up to 100 aircraft. In September 1976 Congress announced the sale to Iran of 160, costing $3·8 billion; it is doubtful that Iran can participate in manufacture. In December 1976 the first of eight development aircraft flew at Fort Worth, and delivery to the USAF is to begin in August 1978. Up to October 1976 $286 million had paid for basic development and flight test; Fiscal Year 1977 voted $620 million for the first 16 production aircraft, and FY78 is expected to provide $1,128 million. USAF buy in the next four years (1978-81) is planned to be 89, 145, 175 and 180, a total to that date of 605. First flight in Europe is planned to be at Schiphol (Fokker-VFW, Amsterdam) in July 1979.

Above: An F-16A development aircraft (curiously, without tail number visible) with nose-mounted instrumentation and tandem triple-ejector racks each carrying two pairs of bombs only.

General Dynamics
F-106 Delta Dart

F-106A and F-106B

Origin: General Dynamics/Convair, USA.
Type: (F-106A) single-seat all-weather interceptor; (F-106B) operational trainer.
Engine: One 24,500lb (11,130kg) thrust Pratt & Whitney J75-17 two-shaft afterburning turbojet.
Dimensions: Span 38ft 3½in (11·67m); length (both) 70ft 8¾in (21·55m); height 20ft 3¼in (6·15m).
Weights: (A) empty 23,646lb (10,725kg); maximum loaded 38,250lb (17,350kg).
Performance: (Both) maximum speed 1,525mph (2455km/h, Mach 2·31); initial climb about 30,000ft (9144m)/min; service ceiling 57,000ft (17,375m); range with drop tanks (A) 1,700 miles (2735km); combat radius, about 600 miles (966km).
Armament: One internal 20mm M-61 multi-barrel cannon; internal weapon bay for air-to-air guided missiles, with typical load comprising one AIR-2A and one AIR-2G Genie rockets and two each of AIM-4E, -4F or 4G Falcons.
History: First flight (aerodynamic prototype) 26 December 1956; (F-106B) 9 April 1958, production delivery July 1959 to July 1960.
User: USA (ANG, USAF).

Development: Originally designated F-102B, the 106 was a natural development of the F-102A with new engine and avionics. By redesigning from scratch to the supersonic Area Rule the fuselage was made much neater and more efficient than that of the earlier aircraft and the more powerful engine resulted in a peak speed approximately twice as fast. The Hughes MA-1 fire control, though no bulkier or heavier than that of the 102, was far more capable and integrated with the SAGE (Semi-Automatic Ground Environment) defence system covering the continental United States in an

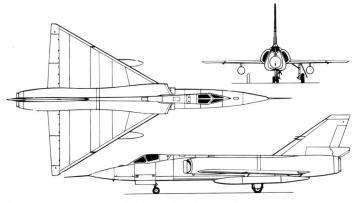

Above: Three-view of F-106A with drop tanks.

automatic manner, the pilot acting as a supervisory manager. Though bought in modest numbers, the 106 has had an exceptionally long life-span in the USAF Aerospace Defense Command front-line inventory. At several times the Improved Manned Interceptor program (IMI) has pointed the need for a replacement with longer-range look-down radar and long-range missiles, and much research has been done with the Lockheed YF-12 (described later). At present no replacement, other than the multi-role F-15, is in sight and the F-106 and tandem-seat F-106B force (respectively numbering originally 277 and 63) will continue until at least 1980. They have been repeatedly updated, with improved avionics, infra-red sensors, drop tanks, flight refuelling and a Gatling gun.

Left: An F-106A Delta Dart of the 460th FIS, a unit later withdrawn from the Aerospace Defense Command active inventory. Despite repeated updating these well-liked interceptors are beginning to show their age, and plans dating back to the late 1960s for their replacement involved special versions of F-15 and F-14.

Left: A recent photograph of one of the remaining F-106A all-weather interceptors, which equip six home-based Air Divisions each comprising a single 18-aircraft squadron.

Below: The meagre regular defensive force is bolstered by Air National Guard units; this Dart comes from the 194th FIS.

43

General Dynamics F-111

"TFX", F-111A to F-111F, EF-111A and FB-111A

Origin: General Dynamics/Fort Worth (EF-111A, Grumman Aerospace), USA.

Type: Two-seat all-weather attack bomber; (EF) two-seat electronic warfare; (FB) two-seat strategic bomber.

Engines: Two Pratt & Whitney TF30 two-shaft afterburning turbofans, at following ratings: (F-111A, C) TF30-3 at 18,500lb (8390kg); (D, E) TF30-9 at 19,600lb (8891kg); (F) RF30-100 at 25,100lb (11,385kg); (FB) TF30-7 at 20,350lb (9230kg).

Dimensions: Span, 72·5° sweep (A, D, E, F) 31ft 11½in (9·74m); (C, FB) 33ft 11in (10·34m); span, 16° sweep (A, D, E, F) 63ft (19·2m); (C, FB) 70ft (21·34m); length 73ft 6in (22·4m); height 17ft 1½in (5·22m).

Weights: Empty (A, C) 46,172lb (20,943kg); (D, E, F) about 49,000lb (22,226kg); (FB) about 50,000lb (22,680kg); maximum loaded (A, 3) 91,500lb (41,500kg); (D, E, F) 99,000lb (44,906kg); (FB) 119,000lb (54,000kg).

Performance: Maximum speed (clean), Mach 2·2 at 35,000ft or above, or about 1,450mph (2335km/h); maximum speed at low level (clean) Mach 1·2 or 800mph (1287km/h); maximum speed at maximum weight, subsonic at low level; service ceiling (clean) (A) 51,000ft (15,500m); (F) 60,000ft (18,290m); range on internal fuel (A, C) 3,165 miles (5093km).

Armament: Internal bay for two 750lb (341kg) bombs or 20mm M-61 multi-barrel gun; eight underwing pylons for total of 31,500lb (14,290kg) of stores, inner pylons swivelling with wing sweep and outer four being fixed and loaded only with wing at 16°.

History: First flight 21 December 1964; service delivery June 1967; first F-111F with -100 engine, May 1973; EF-111A (Grumman ECM conversion) 1977.

Users: Australia, US Air Force.

continued ▶

Below: An unusual view of an F-111E, an interim version basically similar to the original F-111A but with enlarged engine inlet ducts (for a more powerful version of the TF30 afterburning turbofan which was never fitted). The main unit equipped with this sub-type is the 20th TFW based at RAF Upper Heyford, in England. Aircraft in normal operational service have a black radome, unlike that of this aircraft which was on test missions in the United States. Even today the F-111 is the only true all-weather tactical aircraft in service, apart from the US Navy A-6.

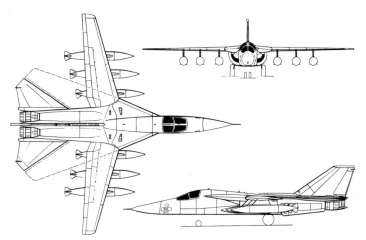

Above: Three-view of the FB-111A strategic bomber version.

Above: A gaily-painted development prototype of the EF-111A all-weather electronic-warfare aircraft, with canoe (belly) and fin aerials for the ALQ-99 EW (Electronic Warfare) installation. The EF-111A programme is being handled chiefly by Grumman.

Below: Considerably more powerful than any other type of F-111, the F-111F is an excellent aircraft in all respects. All the examples of this sub-type in combat duty are serving with the 48th Tactical Fighter Wing at RAF Lakenheath, England, where this photograph was taken in 1979 during training missions.

Development: Developed to meet a bold Department of Defense edict that a common type of "fighter" called TFX should be developed to meet all future tactical needs of all US services, the F-111A proved both a world-beater and a great disappointment. Thrown into the public eye by acrimonious disagreement over which bidder should get the production contract, it then stayed in the news through being grossly overweight, up in drag and suffering from severe problems with propulsion, structure and systems. Eventually almost superhuman efforts cleared the F-111A for service, overcoming part of the range deficiency by a considerable increase in internal fuel. The RAAF bought 24 F-111C with long-span wings and stronger landing gear and took delivery after they had been nine years in storage. The RAF ordered 50 similar to the C but with updated avionics, but this deal was cancelled. Only 141 low-powered A-models were built, the US Navy F-111B fighter was cancelled, and the next batch was 94 of the E type with improved intakes and engines (20th Tac Ftr Wing at Upper Heyford, England). Then came the 96 F-111D with improved avionics (27th TFW in New Mexico) and finally the superb F-111F with redesigned P-100 engine of greatly increased thrust and cheaper avionics (366 TFW, in Idaho). The heavier FB-111A, with the ability to carry six AGM-69A SRAM missiles externally, was bought to replace the B-58 and early B-52 models in Strategic Air Command. Cost-inflation cut the FB order from 210 back to 76. With several RF and ECM conversions the total programme amounted to 539 plus 23 development prototypes. To keep the line open a further 12 were authorised in 1974 to be built at a low rate until 1976. In 1979 the only work on F-111s was structural improvement of aircraft in service and Grumman's conversion of surplus F-111As to EF-111A standard with the ALQ tac-jamming system of the EA-6B Prowler but without extra crew. Despite lack of funds it is hoped to rebuild 40 aircraft of this type to equip two USAF squadrons. The EF will not carry weapons, and will direct other aircraft. No aircraft has ever had worse luck or a worse press, and in combat in South East Asia the sudden loss of three of the first six aircraft was eventually found to be due to a faulty weld in the tailplane power unit. In fact all models of the F-111 are valuable machines with great range and endurance, excellent reliability and great ability to hit a point target in a first-pass strike, even in blind conditions. These aircraft are bombers, with much greater power and weight than four-engined bombers of World War II. It was unfortunate they were loosely launched as "fighters".

Left: Apart from the much older and probably more vulnerable B-52 the only American strategic bomber is the FB-111A, one of which is seen here about to take fuel from a KC-135 tanker. It is carrying its usual armament of four SRAM missiles on the external pylons; if necessary a further two can be accommodated in an internal bay plus two (rarely, four) more on additional wing pylons.

Below: Since the early 1970s General Dynamics has been proposing 'stretched' versions of the FB-111A as a new strategic bomber for USAF Strategic Air Command. This artist's impression shows the FB-111H, with longer fuselage, much greater fuel capacity, bogie main landing gears and two General Electric F101 engines (the same as used in the cancelled B-1 bomber). It would have been an extremely formidable aircraft with much greater radius of action than the somewhat limited FB-111A but was never built.

Grumman A-6 Intruder and Prowler

Grumman A-6A, B, C, E, EA-6A and B and KA-6D

Origin: Grumman Aerospace, USA.

Type: (A-6A, B, C, E) two-seat carrier-based all-weather attack; (EA-6A) two-seat ECM/attack; (EA-6B) four-seat ECM; (KA-6D) two-seat air-refuelling tanker.

Engines: (Except EA-6B) two 9,300lb (4218kg) thrust Pratt & Whitney J52-8A two-shaft turbojets; (EA-6B) two 11,200lb (5080kg) J52-408.

Dimensions: Span 53ft (16·15m); length (except EA-6B) 54ft 7in (16·64m); (EA-6B) 59ft 5in (18·11m); height (A-6A, A-6C, KA-6D) 15ft 7in (4·75m); (A-6E, EA-6A and B) 16ft 3in (4·95m).

Weights: Empty (A-6A) 25,684lb (11,650kg); (EA-6A) 27,769lb (12,596kg); (EA-6B) 34,581lb (15,686kg); (A-6E) 25,630lb (11,625kg); maximum loaded (A-6A and E) 60,626lb (27,500kg); (EA-6A) 56,500lb (25,628kg); (EA-6B) 58,500lb (26,535kg).

Performance: Maximum speed (clean A-6A) 685mph (1102km/h) at sea level or 625mph (1006km/h, Mach 0·94) at height; (EA-6A) over 630mph; (EA-6B) 599mph at sea level; (A-6E) 648mph (1043km/h) at sea level; initial climb (A-6E, clean) 8,600ft (2621m)/min; service ceiling (A-6A) 41,660ft (12,700m); (A-6E) 44,600ft (13,595m); (EA-6B) 39,000ft (11,582m); range with full combat load (A-6E) 1,077 miles (1733km); ferry range with external fuel (all) about 3,100 miles (4890km).

Armament: All attack versions, including EA-6A, five stores locations each rated at 3,600lb (1633kg) with maximum total load of 15,000lb (6804kg); typical load thirty 500lb (227kg) bombs; (EA-6B, KA-6D) none.

History: First flight (YA2F-1) 19 April 1960; service acceptance of A-6A 1 February 1963; first flight (EA-6A) 1963; (KA-6D) 23 May 1966; (EA-6B) 25 May 1968; (A-6E) 27 February 1970; final delivery 1975.

User: USA (Navy, Marine Corps).

Development: Selected from 11 competing designs in December 1957, the Intruder was specifically planned for first-pass blind attack on point surface targets at night or in any weather. Though area ruled, the aircraft (originally designated A2F) was designed to be subsonic and is powered by two straight turbojets which in the original design were arranged with tilting jetpipes to help give lift for STOL (short takeoff and landing). Despite its considerable gross weight — much more than twice the empty weight and heavier than most of the heavy World War II four-engine brombers—the

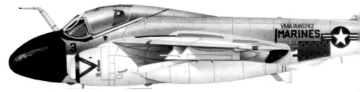

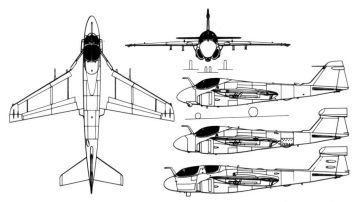

Above: Three-view of A-6E, with side views of EA-6A (centre) and EA-6B (bottom).

Intruder has excellent slow-flying qualities with full span slats and flaps. The crew sit side-by-side under a broad sliding canopy giving a marvellous view in all directions, the navigator having control of the extremely comprehensive navigation, radar and attack systems which are integrated into DIANE (Digital Integrated Attack Navigation Equipment). In Vietnam the A-6A worked round the clock making pinpoint attacks on targets which could not be accurately bombed by any other aircraft until the arrival of the F-111. The A-6E introduced a new multi-mode radar and computer and supplanted earlier versions in Navy and Marine Corps squadrons. The EA-6A introduced a valuable group of ECM (electronic countermeasures), while retaining partial attack capability, but the extraordinary EA-6B is a totally redesigned four-seat aircraft where the entire payload comprises the most advanced and comprehensive ECM equipment ever fitted to a tactical aircraft, part of it being carried in four external pods with windmill generators to supply electric power. The latest addition to attack versions was TRAM (Target Recognition Attack Multisensor), a turreted electro-optical/infra-red system matched with laser-guided weapons. In 1977 Grumman was building new Prowlers and the last A-6Es, and converting A-6A models to the latest E standard. In the course of 1977 the first Intruders were to be modified to fire the Harpoon active-seeker missile.

Left: An A-6E Intruder of a crack Marine unit, VMA(AW)-242, popularly called 'The Bats'.

Below left: Together with a handful of USAF F-111As the Grumman A-6 series were the only tactical aircraft able to operate at night or in bad weather during the tragic war in Vietnam. These A-6As from USS *Constellation* are seen each laying down a dozen 1,000lb retarded bombs.

Below: A-6A trials aircraft from Naval Ordnance Test Station carrying Condor missile.

49

Grumman F-14 Tomcat

F-14A, B and C

Origin: Grumman Aerospace, USA.

Type: Two-seat carrier-based multi-role fighter.

Engines: (F-14A) two 20,900lb (9480kg) thrust Pratt & Whitney TF30-412A two-shaft afterburning turbofans; (B and C) two 28,090lb (12,741kg) thrust Pratt & Whitney F401-400 two-shaft afterburning turbofans.

Dimensions: Span (68° sweep) 38ft 2in (11·63m), (20° sweep) 64ft 1½in (19·54m); length 61ft 2in (18·89m); height 16ft (4·88m).

Weights: Empty 37,500lb (17,010kg); loaded (fighter mission) 55,000lb (24,948kg), (maximum) 72,000lb (32,658kg).

Performance: Maximum speed, 1,564mph (2517km/h, Mach 2·34) at height, 910mph (1470km/h, Mach 1·2) at sea level; initial climb at normal gross weight, over 30,000ft (9144m)/min; service ceiling over 56,000ft (17,070m); range (fighter with external fuel) about 2,000 miles (3200km).

Armament: One 20mm M61-A1 multi-barrel cannon in fuselage; four AIM-7 Sparrow and four or eight AIM-9 Sidewinder air-to-air missiles, or up to six AIM-54 Phoenix and two AIM-9; maximum external weapon load in surface attack role 14,500lb (6577kg).

History: First flight 21 December 1970; initial deployment with US Navy carriers October 1972; first flight of F-14B 12 September 1973.

Users: Iran (available for sale), USA (Navy, Marine Corps).

Development: When Congress finally halted development of the compromised F-111B version of the TFX in mid-1968 Grumman was already well advanced with the project design of a replacement. After a competition for the VFX requirement Grumman was awarded a contract for the F-14 in January 1969. The company had to produce a detailed mock-up by May and build 12 development aircraft. Despite sudden loss of the first aircraft on its second flight, due to total hydraulic failure, the programme has been a complete technical success and produced one of the world's outstanding

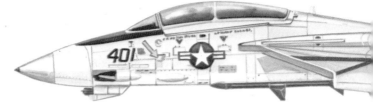

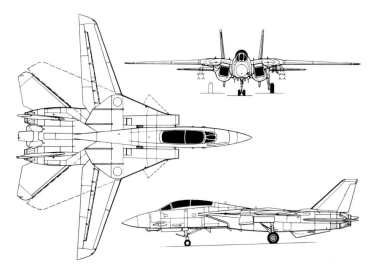

Above: Three-view of an F-14A showing (broken lines) range of wing and glove movement.

combat aircraft. Basic features include use of a variable-sweep wing, to match the aircraft to the conflicting needs of carrier compatability, dog-fighting and attack on surface targets at low level; pilot and naval flight officer (observer) in tandem; an extremely advanced airframe, with tailplane skins of ►

Below: One of the first F-14A Tomcats to be delivered was this example for VF-124 (conversion squadron) at Miramar.

Left: In US markings but customer's camouflage, this F-14A was one of a batch of 80 bought by Iran and delivered before the Shah went into exile in early 1979. Since then the entire force has been non-operational, and has been announced as up for sale. The US government doubts that security of its advanced radar and missile system can have been preserved.

Above: Menacing aspect of an F-14A of US Navy crack fighter squadron VF-211, showing all three missile types on board.

Right: F-14A with everything revealed, including the AWG-9 flat-plate antenna and (foreground) the long-range Phoenix AAM.

Below: Launch of Phoenix from an F-14A detached to Point Mugu.

boron-epoxy composite and similar novel construction methods, and one canted vertical tail above each engine; and the extremely powerful Hughes AWG-9 radar which, used in conjunction with the Phoenix missile (carried by no other combat aircraft), can pick out and destroy a chosen aircraft from a formation at a distance of 100 miles. For close-in fighting the gun is used in conjunction with snap-shoot missiles, with the tremendous advantage that, as a launch platform, the Tomcat is unsurpassed (Grumman claim it to be unrivalled, and to be able – by automatic variation of wing sweep – to out-manoeuvre all previous combat aircraft). Introduction to the US Navy has been smooth and enthusiastic, with VF-1 and -2 serving aboard *Enterprise* in 1974. The export appeal of the F-14 is obvious and Iran is introducing 80 from 1976. But costs have run well beyond prediction, Grumman refusing at one time to continue the programme and claiming its existing contracts would result in a loss of $105 million. For the same reason the re-engined F-14B has been confined to two re-engined A-models, and the F-14C with new avionics and weapons remains a paper project. In 1975 production agreements were worked out and by 1977 total deliveries amounted to 243 aircraft, including about 12 for Iran. The US Navy (which includes the aircraft for the Marines) has funds for 306 F-14As and plans to buy 403 by 1981, but the requirement for an eventual total of over 500 is likely to be cut back as the F-18 comes into production. In 1976 severe trouble hit the F-14, affecting engines, fuselage structure, computer/weapon system and accidents attributed to pilot error. Efforts are being made to improve the operational-readiness rate and, if possible, increase installed engine thrust.

HSA (BAe) Buccaneer

Buccaneer S.1, 2, 2A, 2B, 2C, 2D and 50

Origin: Hawker Siddeley Aviation (formerly Blackburn Aircraft, now British Aerospace), UK.

Type: Two-seat attack and reconnaissance.

Engines: (S.1) two 7,100lb (3220kg) thrust Bristol Siddeley (previously de Havilland) Gyron Junior 101 single-shaft turbojets; (all later marks) two 11,030lb (5003kg) Rolls-Royce Spey 101 two-shaft turbofans.

Dimensions: Span (1) 42ft 4in (12·9m); (2 and subsequent) 44ft (13·41m); length 63ft 5in (19·33m); height 16ft 3in (4·95m).

Weights: Empty (1) 26,000lb (2) about 30,000lb (13,610kg); maximum loaded (1) 46,000lb (20,865kg); (2) 62,000lb (28,123kg).

Performance: Maximum speed (all) 645mph (1038km/h, Mach 0·85) at sea level; initial climb (2, at 46,000lb) 7,000ft (2134m)/min; service ceiling not disclosed but over 40,000ft (9144m); range on typical hi-lo-hi strike mission with weapon load (2) 2,300 miles (3700km).

Armament: Rotating bomb door carries four 1,000lb (454kg) bombs or multi-sensor reconnaissance pack or 440gal tank; (S.2 and later) four wing pylons each stressed to 3,000lb (1361kg), compatible with very wide range of guided and/or free-fall missiles. Total internal and external stores load 16,000lb (7257kg).

History: First flight (NA.39) 30 April 1958; (production S.1) 23 January 1962; (prototype S.2) 17 May 1963; (production S.2) 5 June 1964; final delivery late 1975.

Users: S Africa, UK (RAF, Royal Navy).

Development: After the notorious "Defence White Paper" of April 1957, which proclaimed manned combat aircraft obsolete, the Blackburn B.103, built to meet the naval attack specification NA.39, was the only new British military aircraft that was not cancelled. Development was grudgingly permitted, and this modest-sized subsonic machine was gradually recognised as a world-beater. Designed for carrier operation, its wing and tail were dramatically reduced in size as a result of very powerful tip-to-tip supercirculation (BLC, boundary-layer control) achieved by blasting hot compressed air bled from the engines from narrow slits. The S.1 (strike Mk 1) was marginal on power, but the greatly improved S.2 was a reliable and formidable aircraft. The first 84 were ordered by the Royal Navy and most of these have been transferred to RAF Strike Command, designated S.2B when converted to launch Martel missiles. Those remaining with the Navy are S.2Ds (2C if they are not Martel-compatible). In January 1963 the South African Air Force bought 16 S.50s with BS.605 boost rocket built into a retractable pack in the rear fuselage to facilitate use from hot and high airstrips. Finally — perhaps rather surprisingly, considering the scorn vented on Buccaneer during the TSR.2 era — the RAF signed in 1968 for 43 new S.2Bs with adequate equipment, including a refuelling probe which is never used in front-line service in Germany. Within the limits of crippling budgets the RAF Buccaneers have been updated by improved avionics and ECM, and all

Below: A Buccaneer S.2B of RAF No 16 Sqn which, with No 15, forms the attack/strike force of RAF Germany based at Laarbruch.

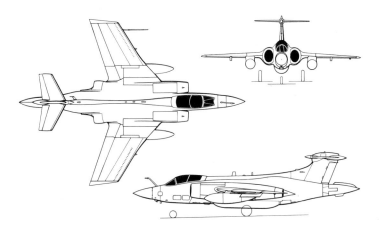

Three-view of Buccaneer S.2 with FR probe and bomb-door tank.

models have the advantage of an unbreakable long-life airframe and the ability to carry weapons internally In 1977 they were getting Pave Spike laser-guided bomb systems. Altogether the Mk 2 Buccaneer is one of the most cost/effective aircraft ever designed for tactical use.

Above: This Buccaneer is seen with its rotary weapon-bay door open, revealing the internal bay which enables it to attack in the clean condition at speeds higher than the maximum speed at sea level of many so-called supersonic attack aircraft (which can reach super- sonic speed only at high altitude and carry their weapons outside).

HSA (BAe) Harrier and Sea Harrier

Harrier GR.3 and T.4, AV-8A, TAV-8A and Sea Harrier FRS.1

Origin: Hawker Siddeley Aviation (now British Aerospace), UK.
Type: Single-seat tactical attack and reconnaissance; (T.4, TAV) dual trainer or special missions; (Sea Harrier) single-seat ship-based multi-role.
Engine: One 21,500lb (9752kg) thrust Rolls-Royce Pegasus 103 two-shaft vectored-thrust turbofan (US designation F402); (Sea H, Pegasus 104).
Dimensions: Span 25ft 3in (7·7m), (with bolt-on tips, 29ft 8in); length 45ft 6in (13·87m), (laser nose, 47ft 2in; two-seat trainers, 55ft 9½in; Sea Harrier, 48ft); height 11ft 3in (3·43m) (two-seat, 13ft 8in).
Weights: Empty (GR.1) 12,200lb (5533kg); (Sea H) 13,000lb (5897kg); (T) 13,600lb (6168kg); maximum (non-VTOL) 26,000lb (11,793kg).
Performance: Maximum speed .737mph (1186km/h, Mach 0·972) at low level; maximum dive Mach number, 1·3; initial climb (VTQL weight) 50,000ft (15,240m)/min; service ceiling, over 50,000ft (15,240m); tactical radius on strike mission without drop tanks (hi-lo-hi) 260 miles (418km); ferry range 2,070 miles (3330km).
Armament: All external, with many options. Under-fuselage strakes both replaceable by pod containing one 30mm Aden or similar gun, with 150 rounds. Five or seven stores pylons, centre and two inboard each rated at 2,000lb (907kg), outers at 650lb (295kg) and tips (if used) at 220lb (100kg) for Sidewinder or similar. Normal load 5,300lb (2400kg), but 8,000lb (3630kg) has been flown.

Below: Unlike every other combat aeroplane in Western Europe the Harrier could escape the devastating missile attack on airfields that would begin any future war in Europe. Unfortunately most Harriers are usually at risk on airfields, instead of being safely dispersed into the countryside as are these Harrier FGA.3 single-seaters pictured during a special exercise in off-base operation.

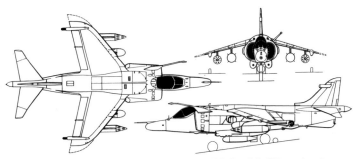

Above: Three-view drawing of Harrier GR.3 with FR probe, laser nose and (dotted) ferry tips.

History: First hover (P.1127) 21 October 1960; first flight (P.1127) 13 March 1961; first flight (Kestrel) 13 February 1964; (development Harrier) 31 August 1966; (Harrier GR.1) 28 December 1967; (T.2) 24 April 1969; (Sea Harrier FRS.1) 20 August 1978; squadron service (GR.1) 1 April 1969; (Sea Harrier) late 1979.

Users: Spain (Navy, AV-8A), UK (RAF, Royal Navy), USA (Marine Corps).

Development: In the 1950s the realisation that the thrust/weight ratio of the gas turbine made possible a new class of high-speed jets having VTOL (vertical takeoff and landing) capability led to a rash of unconventional

continued ▶

Left: Though they are basic attack platforms without most of the sophisticated systems carried by RAF Harriers, the AV-8A Harrier of the US Marine Corps had the important effect of showing an insular Washington that foreign equipment could offer new capabilities. In turn, the Marines explored Harriers as fighters.

Below: A Harrier GR.3 of the RAF salvoes rockets in a firing pass against a ground target. This particular example is armed with four Matra 155 pods, each containing 19 SNEB rockets of 68mm calibre. They are reasonably effective against hardened targets such as armour, though probably not as lethal as the BL.755 cluster bomb which is an alternative now available.

58

By using an upward-curving 'ski jump' a Sea Harrier (or any other STOL aircraft) can carry much heavier loads with complete pilot safety, especially in operations from surface ships. This ski jump was built by Fairey Engineering from existing Medium Girder Bridge components and used at the 1978 Farnborough Air Show for Harriers and (as shown here) the first Sea Harrier FRS.1. Today the Sea Harrier is in service with the Royal Navy and will be deployed aboard the *Invincible*-class light multi-role carriers. *Invincible* has a 7° ramp, while her two sisters, *Illustrious* and *Ark Royal,* have 15° ramps and a relocated Sea Dart launcher.

prototypes and research machines. Only one has led to a useful combat aircraft. It was the P.1127, designed by Camm's team in 1957-59 around a unique engine, planned at Bristol by Stanley Hooker, in which the fan and core flows are discharged through four nozzles which, by means of chain drives from a single pneumatic motor, can be swivelled to point downwards, to lift the aircraft, or point to the rear, for propulsion. Gradually the P.1127 was transformed into the Kestrel, which equipped a UK/USA/German evaluation squadron in 1965. This was further developed into the Harrier (the much bigger, Mach 2, P.1154 for the RAF and RN having been cancelled in 1965). Powered by a Pegasus 101 rated at 19,000lb, the GR.1 was capable of flying useful combinations of fuel and stores out of any hastily prepared site and did more than any other aircraft to explore the advantages and problems of operational deployment of combat aircraft well away from any airfield. Numerous flights were made from a wide variety of naval vessels and record flights were made from the centre of London to the centre of New York and vice versa. The GR.1A had the 20,000lb Mk 102 engine and at this thrust the Harrier was adopted as the AV-8A by the US Marine Corps in both beach assault and defensive roles. All RAF and USMC aircraft have been re-engined with the Pegasus 103, giving a payload/range performance adequate for a wide spectrum of missions, many of which cannot be flown by any other aircraft. Using VIFF (vectoring in forward flight) the Harrier can fly "impossible" manoeuvres and has proved itself an extremely tricky customer in a dogfight. This is not its main mission, however, and the RAF Harrier GR.3 (92 built) is primarily a tactical attack platform with Ferranti INAS (inertial nav/attack system) and laser ranger. The USMC AV-8A (112, plus six for Spain named Matador) does not have either of these equipments but carries Sidewinder air/air missiles. Including two-seaters, production by 1977 amounted to 231. In Britain the main effort is completing development of the redesigned Sea Harrier, which should fly in 1977. The Royal Navy will deploy 24 from throughdeck cruisers and possibly other ships, and several other navies are discussing possible orders. The Sea Harrier has a completely new nose, with raised cockpit, Blue Fox radar, much enhanced systems and equipment and weapons for surface attack, reconnaissance, anti-submarine warfare and air combat. Since 1975 talks have been held with China, which is interested in buying a large number of Harriers. The next-generation AV-8B is discussed under McDonnell Douglas.

Below: A fine portrait of a British Aerospace TAV-8A Harrier dual-control trainer (with full combat capability) of the US Marine Corps, serving with VMAT-203, which handles the important task of converting pilots for VMA-231, -513 and -542.

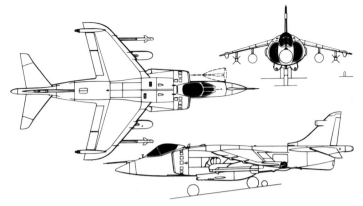

Above: Three-view drawing of Sea Harrier FRS.1.

Below: A British Aerospace Sea Harrier FRS.1, which entered service in autumn 1979 with 700A Sqn, the RN Intensive Flying Trials Unit at RNAS Yeovilton. In 1980 these extremely versatile multi-role aircraft embarked aboard HMS *Invincible*.

HSA (BAe) Hawk

P.1182 Hawk T.1

Origin: British Aerospace, UK.
Type: Two-seat trainer and tactical multi-role.
Engine: One 5,340lb (2422kg) Rolls-Royce/Turboméca Adour 151 two-shaft turbofan.
Dimensions: Span 30ft 10in (9·4m); length (over probe) 39ft 2½in (11·95m); height 13ft 5in (4·09m).
Weights: Empty 7,450lb (3379kg); loaded (trainer, clean) 12,000lb (5443kg), (attack mission) 16,260lb (7375kg).
Performance: Maximum speed 630mph (1014km/h) at low level; Mach number in shallow dive, 1·1; initial climb 6,000ft (1830m)/min; service ceiling 50,000ft (15,240m); range on internal fuel 750 miles (1207km); endurance with external fuel 3 hr.
Armament: Three or five hard-points (two outboard being optional) each rated at 1,000lb (454kg); centreline point normally equipped with 30mm gun pod and ammunition.
History: First flight 21 August 1974; service delivery 1976.
Users: Finland, Indonesia, Kenya, UK (RAF).

Development: The only new all-British military aircraft for 15 years, the Hawk serves as a model of the speed and success that can be achieved when an experienced team is allowed to get on with the job. To some degree it owes its existence to the escalation of the Jaguar to a power and weight category well above that economic for use as a pure trainer. Britain never participated in the Franco-German Alpha Jet programme and instead played off the two British airframe builders, finally making a choice between the Adour without afterburner and the less powerful Viper 632. With the Adour, the Hawk had a chance to be a world-beater, and backed by an immediate RAF order for 175 the Hawker Siddeley plants rapidly completed design, tooled for fast manufacture with assembly at Dunsfold and completed development of the RAF T.1 version all within the first two years of the programme. By October 1976 a dozen aircraft had flown and deliveries had begun to the RAF to replace the Gnat, Hunter and, eventually, Jet Provost. in roles ranging from basic flying to advanced weapon training. Thanks to very rapid development the Hawk was kept to the original budget and price and by late 1979 nearly all the 175 aircraft for the RAF had been delivered. So pleased is the RAF that a repeat-order has been requested, though funds are awaited. A proportion of Hawks may be single-seat dedicated close-support machines.

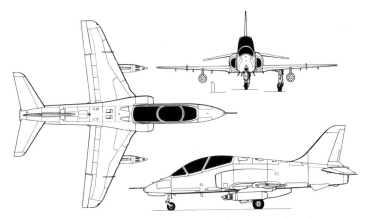

Above: Three-view of Hawk with centreline gun and rockets.

Above: One of approximately 100 Hawk T.1 multi-role advanced trainers serving with 4 Flying Training School at RAF Valley.

Below: In this configuration about 50 Hawks are flying with No 234 Sqn, part of No 1 Tactical Weapons Unit, at RAF Brawdy.

HSA (BAe) Hunter

Hunter 1 to 79

Origin: Hawker Aircraft, UK (now British Aerospace); licence-production in Belgium/Netherlands.

Type: Single-seat fighter, fighter-bomber and fighter-reconnaissance; two-seat dual trainer.

Engine: One Rolls-Royce Avon single-shaft turbojet (see text).

Dimensions: Span 33ft 8in (10·26m); length (single-seat, typical) 45ft 10½in (13·98m), (two-seat) 48ft 10½in (14·9m); height 13ft 2in (4.26m).

Weights: Empty (1) 12,128lb (5501kg); (9) 13,270lb (6020kg); loaded (1) 16,200lb (7347kg); (9, clean) 17,750lb (8051kg); (9, maximum) 24,000lb (10,885kg).

Performance: Maximum speed (typical of all) 710mph (1144km/h) at sea level, 620mph (978km/h, Mach 0·94) at height; initial climb (Avon 100-series) about 5,500ft (1676m)/min; (Avon 200-series) 8,000ft (2438m)/service ceiling 50,000ft (15,240m); range on internal fuel 490 miles (689km), with maximum fuel 1,840 miles (2965km).

Armament: Four (two-seaters, usually one, sometimes two) 30mm Aden cannon beneath cockpit floor, each with 150 rounds; single-seaters normally have underwing pylons for two 1,000lb (454kg) bombs and 24 3in rockets, later or refurbished aircraft carrying two 230 Imp gal drop tanks in addition.

History: First flight (P.1067) 20 June 1951; (production F.1) 16 May 1953; (two-seater) 8 July 1955; final delivery from new, 1966.

Users: Abu Dhabi, Chile, India, Iraq, Kenya, Kuwait, Lebanon, Oman, Peru, Qatar, Singapore, Switzerland, UK (RAF, Royal Navy), Zimbabwe-Rhodesia.

Development: Undoubtedly the most successful British post-war fighter, the Hunter epitomised the grace of a thoroughbred and has always delighted its pilots. The prototype, with 6,500lb thrust Avon 100, was built to Specification F.3/48. It was easily supersonic in a shallow dive and packed the devastating four Aden cannon in a quick-release pack winched up as a unit. After being fitted with bulged cartridge boxes and a stuck-on airbrake under the rear fuselage it became a standard fighter, with Armstrong Whitworth building the F.2 with 8,000lb Sapphire 101, which, unlike the early

Below: A brace of Hunter F.74B single-seaters of the Singapore Air Defence Command, one of the last and most satisfied Hunter customers.

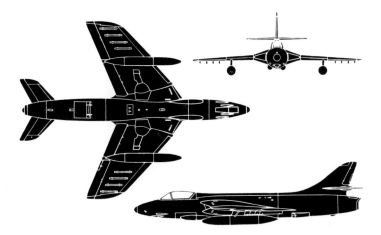

Three-view of Hunter FGA.9, typical of most single-seaters today.

Avon, stayed going when the guns were fired. The one-off Mk 3 gained a world speed record at 727·6mph, the F.4 had fuel capacity raised from 334 to 414 gal and carried underwing stores, and the F.5 was a Sapphire-engined 4. The F.6 introduced the 10,000lb Avon 203 and extended-chord dog-tooth wing. The T.7 had the 8,000lb Avon 122 and side-by-side dual controls, the T.8 was a naval trainer, and the most important mark of all was the FGA.9 with 10,150lb Avon 207 and heavier underwing load. The FR.10 was a camera-equipped fighter and the GA.11 was a ground-attack naval trainer. Total Hunter production was 1,985, including 445 made in Belgium and Holland. While 429 were exported as new aircraft, well over 700 additional Hunters have been refurbished or completely remanufactured for more than 17 air forces, with mark numbers up to 79. A superb all-round combat aircraft, it is gradually being recognised that, had a further 1,000 been constructed (or fewer scrapped in Britain) all would have found ready buyers today.

Left: This Hunter F.51 was one formerly used by the Royal Danish Air Force (724 Sqn).

Below: Takeoff by a Hunter FGA.9 of No 45 Sqn RAF, one of the last units to have operated this outstanding aircraft in Britain.

Hawker Siddeley Gnat/HAL Ajeet

Fo 141 Gnat F.1, HAL Gnat and Ajeet, Hawker Siddeley Gnat T.1

Origin: Folland Aircraft (now British Aerospace), UK; Ajeet, Hindustan Aerospace Ltd, India.

Type: (Gnat 1 and Ajeet) single-seat fighter; (Gnat T.1) advanced trainer.

Engine: (Gnat 1) 4,520lb (2050kg) thrust Rolls-Royce (previously Bristol, then Bristol Siddeley) Orpheus 701 single-shaft turbojet; (Gnat II/Ajeet) 4,670lb (2118kg) HAL-built Orpheus 701E; Gnat T.1, 4,230lb (1920kg) Orpheus 101.

Dimensions: Span (1) 22ft 2in (6·75m); (Ajeet) 22ft 1in (6·73m), (T.1) 24ft (7·32m); length (1) 29ft 9in (9·06m), (Ajeet) 29ft 8in (9·04m), (T.1) 31ft 9in (9·65m); height (1, Ajeet) 8ft 10in (2·69m), (T.1) 10ft 6in (3·2m).

Weights: Empty, (1, Ajeet) typically 4,850lb (2200kg); (T.1) 5,613lb (2546kg); loaded (1, Ajeet, clean) 6,650lb (3016kg); (1, Ajeet, with external stores) 8,885lb (4030kg); (T.1, clean) 8,250lb (3742kg); (T.1, maximum) 9,350lb (4240kg).

Performance: Maximum speed, (F.1) 714mph (1150km/h); (T.1) 636mph (1026km/h); initial climb, (F.1) 20,000ft (6096m)/min; (T.1) 9,850ft (3000m)/min; service ceiling, (F.1) over 50,000ft (15,250m); (T.1) 48,000ft (14,600m); range, all versions, maximum fuel, 1,180 miles (1900km).

Armament: (F.1, Ajeet) two 30mm Aden cannon, each with 115 rounds; four underwing hardpoints for 1,100lb (454kg) total load. (T.1) no guns, but same underwing load.

History: First flight (Fo 139 Midge) 11 August 1954; (Fo 141 Gnat) 18 July 1955; (T.1) 31 August 1959; (HAL Gnat) 18 November 1959; final delivery (HAL) early 1973; Ajeet, continuing.

Users: Finland (not operational), India, UK (T.1).

Development: British designer Teddy Petter planned the Gnat to reverse the trend towards larger and more complex combat aircraft, considering a simple lightweight fighter would offer equal performance at much lower cost. Folland Aircraft built the low-powered (1,640lb Viper) Midge as a private venture and eventually gained an order for a development batch of six, the first of which flew in May 1956. India signed a licence agreement in September 1956 and by early 1973 had built 213 at Hindustan Aerospace (HAL) at Bangalore, as well as receiving 25 Mk 1 Gnats and 25 sets of parts from Folland. HAL also built the Orpheus engine. Finland bought 12, three having a three-camera nose for FR duties, and two were supplied to

Below: The first true HAL Ajeet pictured in formation with a Kiran Mk 1 on a visit to Britain in 1975.

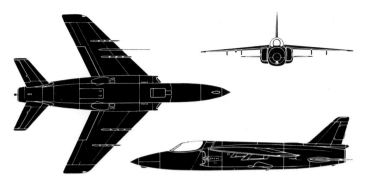

Above: Three-view of the Ajeet, showing four stores pylons.

Jugoslavia. The Gnat was modified into a trainer for the RAF, with tandem cockpits, later wing and many other changes and 105 were supplied by Hawker Siddeley (into which Folland was absorbed) in 1962-65. Smoke-making Gnat T.1s equip the Red Arrows aerobatic team. In 1969 HAL began to study an improved Gnat which was finally agreed in 1974. Named Gnat II or Ajeet (Unconquerable), it has integral-tank wings housing the same quantity of fuel as was formerly carried in underwing tanks, thus allowing full weapon load to be carried for undiminished range; it also has improved avionics and many minor changes. HAL Gnats are progressively being brought up to this standard. In prolonged combat duty the HAL Gnats have acquitted themselves well and proved most effective in close combat.

Below: Nose of a Gnat on the flight line at HAL's Bangalore factory. The fuel in the drop tank is carried inside the Ajeet wing.

Hindustan HF-24 Marut

HAL HF-24 Mk I, IT and II

Origin: Hindustan Aeronautics, India.

Type: Single-seat fighter and ground attack (IT, two-seat trainer).

Engines: Two 4,850lb (2200kg) thrust Rolls-Royce (originally ·Bristol, then Bristol Siddeley) Orpheus 703 single-shaft turbojets, licence-made by HAL.

Dimensions: Span 26ft 6¼in (9m); length 52ft 0¾in (15·87m); height 11ft 9¾in (3·6m).

Weights: (Mk I) empty 13,658lb (6195kg); loaded (clean) 19,734lb (8951kg); loaded (maximum) 24,085lb (10,925kg).

Performance: Maximum speed, 691mph (1112km/h, Mach 0·91) at sea level, about 675mph (1086km/h, Mach 1·02) at altitude; time to climb to 40,000ft (12,200m) 9min 20sec; range on internal fuel about 620 miles (1000km).

Armament: Four 30mm Aden Mk 2 cannon each with 120 rounds, retractable Matra pack of 50 SNEB 68mm rockets, and four wing pylons each rated at 1,000lb (454kg).

History: First flight 17 June 1961; (pre-production) March 1963; (series production) 15 November 1967; (Mk IT) 30 April 1970.

User: India.

Development: After 1950 the Indian government decided to authorise development of an Indian combat aircraft, and the services of Dipl-Ing Kurt Tank, the renowned Focke-Wulf designer, were secured to lead a new team formed by Hindustan Aircraft at Banglore. Detail design began in 1956, the objective being to create a multi-role aircraft potentially capable of reaching Mach 2 with minimal technical risk. The prototype, powered by two of the same engines already being produced for the Gnat, proved generally successful, and two of the 18 pre-production Maruts ("Wind Spirit") were officially handed over (though as a token delivery) to the IAF in May 1964, the year the company reorganised and expanded into its present form as

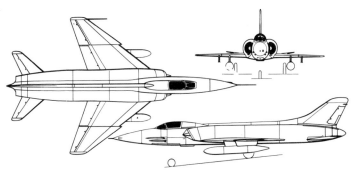

Above: Three-view of HF-24 Marut Mk 1 with drop tanks.

Hindustan Aeronautics. By the end of 1976 about 100 production Mk Is had been delivered, many of them being used (without loss) in the December 1971 war against Pakistan. The Mk IT has a second Martin-Baker seat in place of the rocket pack and has since 1974 also been produced in small numbers as a dual conversion and weapon trainer. In 1967 the German staff left and an Indian design team has since continued the 20-year search for a more powerful engine. HAL has tested afterburning engines and flew the Marut IBX with one Orpheus replaced by an Egyptian Brandner E-300, but the most likely solution will be the HSS-73 (Marut III) with two Turbo-Union RB.199 engines in a considerably improved airframe. Despite obvious handicaps HAL has already created a useful multi-role platform which could carry radar, cameras or other equipment and has reached a satisfactory state of operational development. The Mk III could continue the same basic design to the end of the century.

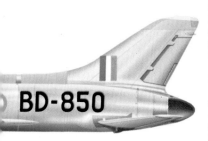

Left: One of the production HF-24 Marut Mk 1 fighter/ attack aircraft, with four guns and underwing drop tanks.

Below: This more recent Mk 1 Marut has noticeably different dielectric (electronics aerial) fairings on the spine and fin, besides having the upper cannon deleted and blanked off.

IAI Kfir

Kfir and Kfir-C2

Origin: Israel Aircraft Industries, Israel.
Type: Single-seat fighter bomber.
Engine: One 17,900lb (8120kg) thrust General Electric J79-17 single-shaft turbojet with afterburner.
Dimensions: Span 26ft 11½in (8·22m); length approximately 54ft (16·5m); height 13ft 11½in (4·25m).
Weights: Empty 14,960lb (6785kg); loaded (fighter mission, half internal fuel, two Shafrir) 20,470lb (9305kg); maximum loaded 32,120lb (14,600kg).
Performance: (Fighter configuration): maximum speed 850mph (1370km/h, Mach 1·12) at sea level, 1,550mph (2495km/h, Mach 2·35) at altitude; initial climb 40,000ft (12,200m)/min; service ceiling, 55,000ft (16,765m); range on internal fuel 700 miles (1125km).
Armament: Two 30mm DEFA 553 cannon, each with 150 rounds; external weapon load up to 8,500lb (3855kg), normally including one ECM pod and two Shafrir air/air missiles.
History: First flight, prior to 1974; service delivery, prior to 1975.
Users: Argentina (Atar-powered Dagger version), Israel.

Development: In the 1950s the beleaguered state of Israel looked principally to France for its combat aircraft and it was mainly with Israeli partnership that Dassault was able to develop the original Mirage IIIC as a combat type. In the fantastic Six-Day War of 5-10 June 1967 the Israeli Mirage IIICJ starred as the most brilliantly flown combat aircraft of modern times; but Dassault was angrily told by Gen de Gaulle not to deliver the improved Mirage 5 attack aircraft which had been developed for Israel and already paid for. With this history it was a foregone conclusion that Israel Aircraft Industries (IAI) at Lod Airport should be directed to apply their great technical expertise to making Israel more self-sufficient in combat aircraft and, in particular, to devising an improved IAI development of the Mirage which could be built in Israel. By 1971 there were reports of a Mirage powered by the J79 engine, supposedly named Barak (Lightning), and such aircraft were even said to have participated in quantity in the 1973 Yom Kippur war. On 14 April 1975 the truth (some of it) escaped when tight Israeli security relented briefly at the public unveiling of the Kfir (Lion Cub). Described as one of the cheapest modern combat aircraft, the Kfir is not a remanufactured IIICJ — though the prototypes were — but a new multi-role fighter bomber making a significant advance over previous delta Mirages. The engine is considerably more powerful and necessitated redesign of the fuselage and addition of a ram-cooling inlet ahead of the fin. The shorter engine results in a shorter rear fuselage, but the nose is much lengthened and equipped with

In the air the gaily painted Kfir-C2 presents a striking appearance, and its aerodynamic improvements confer exceptional manoeuvrability.

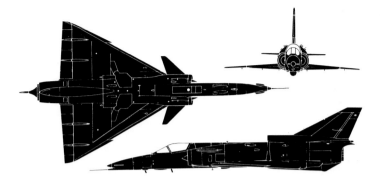

Above: Three-view of IAI Kfir C2.

comprehensive avionics. The entire flight-control and weapon delivery system is by IAI companies and a generation later than that even of the Mirage F1. Though the Kfir did not mature in time to participate in the 1973 war, IAI did clear a number of locally built Atar-powered machines called Neshers which took part in that conflict. The Kfir has continued to develop considerably since entering service in early 1975, and by mid-1976 — when about one-third of the planned force of over 100 were in service — details were released of the Kfir-C2. This incorporates a sharply swept fixed fore-plane above the wing-root leading edge, dogtooth extensions to the outer wings and small fences on each side of the nose. The C2 has improved takeoff and landing and considerably better flight manoeuvrability. All Kfirs are believed to have one autopilot channel with electric "fly by wire" signalling. Production rate is about four per month, and in 1976 IAI announced that it would welcome export orders, at a unit price (without support or spares) of only about $4·5 million. Discussions were then in progress with Austria and certain S. American countries.

Nesher (Eagle)

When General De Gaulle instructed Dassault not to deliver the Mirage 5 aircraft ordered and paid for by Israel, and developed by Dassault specifically for the Israeli Air Force, IAI was assigned the task of making Israel independent of French help. The ultimate result was the Kfir (see above), but as an interim measure IAI produced a copy of the Mirage 5 with Atar 9C engine. The prototype is reported to have flown in October 1969. Deliveries began in 1972, and about 40 Neshers are said to have participated in the October 1973 war.

Jurom VTI/CIAR-93 Orao

VTI-CIAR 93 Orao

Origin: Joint programme by Centrala Industriala Aeronautica Romana, Bucharest, Romania, and Vazduhoplovno-Techniki Institut, Zarkovo, Yugoslavia.

Type: Single-seat tactical attack.

Engines: Two 4,000lb (1814kg) thrust Rolls-Royce/Fiat Viper 632 single-shaft turbojets.

Dimensions: (Estimated) span 24ft 10in (7·56m); length 42ft 4in (12·9m); height 12ft 5in (3·78m).

Weights: (Estimated) empty 9,480lb (4300kg); loaded (fighter mission) 15,875lb (7200kg); maximum loaded 19,850lb (9000kg).

Performance: (Estimated) maximum speed, equivalent to about Mach 0·95 over wide height band (thus, about 700–720mph, 1150km/h, clean at sea level); maximum speed with weapons, about 550mph (885km/h) at sea level; initial climb (clean) at least 15,000ft (4600m)/min; range on internal fuel (clean, high altitude) about 900 miles (1450km).

Armament: Two Nudelmann-Richter NR-30 30mm cannon, each with 125 rounds; centreline and underwing hardpoints, each reported to be rated at 500kg (maximum total external load, 4,840lb, 2200kg) for wide range of Yugoslav cluster bombs, frag bombs, h.e. and napalm (some retarded), rocket pods (12×57mm) or photoflashes.

History: Start of design 1971; first flight believed August 1974; official demonstration 15 April 1975; service delivery, probably December 1976.

Users: Romania, Yugoslavia.

Development: In 1971 the governments of Romania and Yugoslavia agreed to attempt to meet a common requirement of their air forces for a new tactical combat aircraft by building their own. The decision was specifically aimed to help the two countries become more independent of what had previously been a unique source of military equipment. It is significant that the necessary technical help to carry out what was a most challenging project for the two countries came from the West, especially from the UK (which provides engines and most of the airborne system-hardware, and has probably also assisted with the design and development phases). As no bilateral management organization has been announced observers call the project the "Jurom" (Jugoslavia/Romania), but its correct designation is given above (Orao means eagle).

Above: Three-view of Orao prototype as at first showing in 1975.

The aircraft is intended to fulfil several important roles, especially tactical interdiction, close-air support (with laser ranger) and multi-sensor reconnaissance. A two-seat version is among the development batch of 11 aircraft, and several of these roles are judged to need a second crew-member (despite the payload/range limitation with aircraft of modest power). The two-seater will also fulfil the need for a trainer more advanced than the Soko Galeb. Later it is hoped to produce a fighter version, with afterburning engines and a lightweight multimode radar. From the start the Orao has been planned to operate from unpaved and relatively short airstrips, though the early pre-production machines did not have the expected slats and double-slotted flaps (but they did have a braking chute and soft-field tyres). By 1977 it was reported that all 11 development aircraft had flown (apparently some assembled in each country, but all bearing the joint VTI-CIAR designation) and that production deliveries were about to begin. If the partners achieve their objective of export sales it may enable work to go ahead on a modern air-combat fighter version with a restressed airframe, and possibly canards, twin vertical tails and double-shock variable inlets. There appears to be the potential in this joint effort for long-term competition for both East and West.

Below: The first Orao prototype, which flew in 1974. Since then development has been rather slow, though in 1980 it was believed that two further prototypes and nine pre-production machines (including a dual two-seater) were in the air. No announcement has been made by Rolls-Royce regarding a planned afterburning version of the Viper 632 for production Oraos.

Lockheed F-104 Starfighter

F-104A to G, J and S, CF-104, QF-104, RF and RTF-104, TF-104 (data for F-104G)

Origin: Lockheed-California Co, USA; see text for multinational manufacturing programme.

Type: (A, C) single-seat day interceptor; (G) multimission strike fighter; (CF) strike-reconnaissance; (TF) dual trainer; (QF) drone RPV; (F-104S) all-weather interceptor; (RF and RTF) reconnaissance.

Engine: One General Electric J79 single-shaft turbojet with afterburner; (A) 14,800lb (6713kg) J79-3B; (C, D, F, J) 15,800lb (7165kg) J79-7A; (G, RF/RFT, CF) 15,800lb (7165kg) J79-11A; (S) 17,900lb (8120kg) J79-19 or J1Q.

Dimensions: Span (without tip tanks) 21ft 11in (6·68m); length 54ft 9in (16·69m); height 13ft 6in (4·11m).

Weights: Empty 14,082lb (6387kg); maximum loaded 28,779lb (13,054kg).

Performance: Maximum speed 1,450mph (2330km/h, Mach 2·2); initial climb 50,000ft (15,250m)/min; service ceiling 58,000ft (17,680m) (zoom ceiling over 90,000ft, 27,400m); range with maximum weapons, about 300 miles (483km); range with four drop tanks (high altitude, subsonic) 1,380 miles (2220km).

Armament: In most versions, centreline rack rated at 2,000lb (907kg) and two underwing pylons each rated at 1,000lb (454kg); additional racks for small missiles (eg Sidewinder) on fuselage, under wings or on tips; certain versions have reduced fuel and one 20mm M61 Vulcan multi-barrel gun in fuselage; (S) M61 gun, two Sparrow and two Sidewinder.

History: First flight (XF-104) 7 February 1954; (F-104A) 17 February 1956; (F-104G) 5 October 1960; (F-104S) 30 December 1968; final delivery from United States 1964; final delivery from Aeritalia (F-104S) 1975.

Users: Belgium, Canada, Denmark, W Germany, Greece, Italy, Japan, Jordan, Netherlands, Norway, Pakistan, Spain, Taiwan, Turkey, USA (ANG).

Development: Clarence L. ("Kelly") Johnson planned the Model 83 after talking with fighter pilots in Korea in 1951. The apparent need was for superior flight performance, even at the expense of reduced equipment and other penalties. When the XF-104 flew, powered by a 10,500lb J65 Sapphire with afterburner, it appeared to have hardly any wing; another odd feature was the downward-ejecting seat. The production F-104A had a more powerful engine and blown flaps and after lengthy development entered limited service with Air Defense Command in 1958. Only 153 were

Three-view of F-104S, showing Sparrows and Sidewinders.

built and after a spell with the Air National Guard, survivors again saw ADC service with the powerful GE-19 engine. Three were modified as Astronaut trainers with rocket boost, one gaining a world height record at nearly 119,000ft in 1963. The B was a dual tandem trainer, the C a fighter-bomber for Tactical Air Command with refuelling probe, the D a trainer version of the C and the DJ and F respectively Japanese and German versions of the D. The G was a complete redesign to meet the needs of the Luftwaffe for a tactical nuclear strike and reconnaissance aircraft. Structurally different, it introduced Nasarr multi-mode radar, inertial navigation system, manoeuvring flaps and other new items. Altogether 1,266 were built, including 970 by a NATO European consortium and 110 by Canadair. Canadair also built 200 basically similar CF-104s, while Japan built 207 J models closely resembling the earlier C. The German RF and RTF are multi-role-sensor reconnaissance and trainer versions, while increasing numbers of all versions are being turned into various QF-104 RPVs.

The only type of Starfighter built new since 1967 has been the Italian F-104S. Developed jointly by Lockheed and Fiat (Aeritalia), the S is an air-superiority fighter armed with two Sparrow air/air missiles (hence the suffix-letter S). Built under Lockheed licence, the S has a more powerful J79 engine, updated Autonetics R21G radar (with MTI, ECCM and improved reliability) and several detail changes to improve air/air role performance. The secondary ground-attack capability is retained, and in recent months the Regia Aeronautica force of 205 F-104S have begun to carry the Orpheus multi-sensor reconnaissance pod carried on the centre-line. Turkey has bought 40, followed by a second batch of the same size.

Below: Launching a Kormoran anti-ship missile from an F-104G of the West German Marineflieger. These aircraft are to be replaced by the first IDS Tornados to enter inventory service.

McDonnell Douglas A-4 Skyhawk

A-4A to A-4S and TA-4 series

Origin: Douglas Aircraft Co, El Segundo (now division of McDonnell Douglas, Long Beach), USA.

Type: Single-seat attack bomber; TA, dual-control trainer.

Engine: (B, C. L, P, Q, S) one 7,700lb (3493kg) thrust Wright J65-16A single-shaft turbojet (US Sapphire); (E, J) 8,500lb (3856kg) Pratt & Whitney J52-6 two-shaft turbojet; (F, G, H, K) 9,300lb (4218kg) J52-8A; (M, N) 11,200lb (5080kg) J52-408A.

Dimensions: Span 27ft 6in (8·38m); length (A) 39ft 1in; (B) 39ft 6in (42ft 10¾in over FR probe); (E, F, G, H, K, L, P, Q, S) 40ft 1½in (12·22m); (M, N) 40ft 3¼in (12·27m); (TA series, excluding probe) 42ft 7¼in (12·98m); height 15ft (4·57m); (early single-seaters 15ft 2in, TA series 15ft 3in).

Weights: Empty (A) 7,700lb; (E) 9,284lb; (typical modern single-seat, eg M) 10,465lb (4747kg); (TA-4F) 10,602 (4809kg); maximum loaded (A) 17,000lb; (B) 22,000lb; (all others, shipboard) 24,500lb (11,113kg); (land-based) 27,420lb (12,437kg).

Performance: Maximum speed (clean) (B) 676mph; (E) 685mph; (M) 670mph (1078km/h); (TA-4F) 675mph; maximum speed (4,000lb, 1814kg bomb load) (F) 593mph; (M) 645mph; initial climb (F) 5,620ft (1713m)/min; (M) 8,440ft (2572m)/min; service ceiling (all, clean) about 49,000ft (14,935m); range (clean, or with 4,000lb weapons and max fuel, all late versions) about 920 miles (1480km); maximum range (M) 2,055 miles (3307km).

Armament: Standard on most versions, two 20mm Mk 12 cannon, each with 200 rounds; (H, N, and optional on other export versions) two 30mm DEFA 553, each with 150 rounds. Pylons under fuselage and wings for total ordnance load of (A, B, C) 5,000lb (2268kg); (E, F, G, H, K, L, P, Q, S) 8,200lb (3720kg); (M, N) 9,155lb (4153kg).

History: First flight (XA4D-1) 22 June 1954; (A-4A) 14 August 1954; squadron delivery October 1956; (A-4C) August 1959; (A-4E) July 1961; (A-4F) August 1966; (A-4M) April 1970; (A-4N) June 1972; first of TA series (TA-4E) June 1965.

Users: Argentina, Australia, Israel, Kuwait, New Zealand, Singapore, USA (Air Force in SE Asia, Navy, Marine Corps).

Development: Most expert opinion in the US Navy refused to believe the claim of Ed Heinemann, chief engineer of what was then Douglas El Segundo, that he could build a jet attack bomber weighing half the 30,000lb

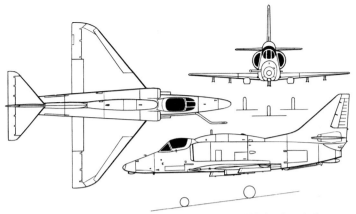

Above: Three-view of McDonnell Douglas A-4M Skyhawk II.

specified by the Navy. The first Skyhawk, nicknamed "Heinemann's Hot Rod", not only flew but gained a world record by flying a 500km circuit at over 695mph. Today, more than 23 years later, greatly developed versions are still in production, setting an unrivalled record for sustained manufacture. These late versions do weigh close to 30,000lb, but only because the basic design has been improved with more powerful engines, increased fuel capacity and much heavier weapon load. The wing was made in a single unit, forming an integral fuel tank and so small it did not need to fold. Hundreds of Skyhawks have served aboard carriers, but in the US involvement in SE Asia "The Scooter" (as it was affectionately known) flew many kinds of mission from land bases. In early versions the emphasis was on improving range and load and the addition of all-weather avionics. The F model introduced the dorsal hump containing additional avionics, and the M, the so-called Skyhawk II, marked a major increase in mission effectiveness. Most of the TA-4 trainers closely resembled the corresponding single-seater, but the TA-4J and certain other models have simplified avionics and the TA-4S (Singapore) is a rebuild by Lockheed Aircraft Service with two separate humped cockpits and an integral-tank fuselage. Production of the M for the US Marine Corps continued in production to the 2,960th Skyhawk in February 1979.

Left: In no country has the Skyhawk seen more combat duty, nor suffered such heavy losses, as Israel. This A-4H (H for Hebrew) is typical of the large force which even today equip six combat-ready Heyl Ha'Avir squadrons.

Below: Launching a Shrike anti-radar missile from a 'Camel' (hump-backed A-4) from US Navy attack squadron VA-55 at the Pacific Missile Range.

77

McDonnell Douglas F-4 Phantom II

F-4A to F-4S, RF-4, QF-4, EF-4

Origin: McDonnell Aircraft, division of McDonnell Douglas Corp, St Louis, USA; licence production by Mitsubishi, Japan (F-4EJ) and substantial subcontracting by W German industry.

Type: Originally carrier-based all-weather interceptor; now all-weather multi-role fighter for ship or land operation; (RF) all-weather multisensor reconnaissance; (QF) RPV; (EF) defence-suppression aircraft.

Engines: (B, G) two 17,000lb (7711kg) thrust General Electric J79-8 single-shaft turbojets with afterburner; (C, D) 17,000lb J79-15; (E, EJ, F) 17,900lb (8120kg) J79-17; (J, N, S) 17,900lb J79-10; (K, M) 20,515lb (9305kg) Rolls-Royce Spey 202/203 two-shaft augmented turbofans.

Dimensions: Span 38ft 5in (11·7m); length (B, C, D, G, J, N, S) 58ft 3in (17·76m); (E, EJ, F and all RF versions) 62ft 11in or 63ft (19·2m); (K, M) 57ft 7in (17·55m); height (all) 16ft 3in (4·96m).

Weights: Empty (B, C, .D, G, J, N) 28,000lb (12,700kg); (E, EJ, F and RF) 29,000lb (13,150kg); (K, M).31,000lb (14,060kg); maximum loaded (B) 54,600lb; (C, D, G, J, K, M, N, RF) 58,000lb (26,308kg); (E, EJ, F) 60,630lb (27,502kg).

Performance: Maximum speed with Sparrow missiles only (low) 910mph (1464km/h, Mach 1·19) with J79 engines, 920mph with Spey, (high) 1,500mph (2414km/h, Mach 2·27) with J79 engines, 1,386mph with Spey; initial climb, typically 28,000ft (8534m)/min with J79 engines, 32,000ft/min with Spey; service ceiling, over 60,000ft (19,685m) with J79 engines, 60,000ft with Spey; range on internal fuel (no weapons) about 1,750 miles (2817km); ferry range with external fuel, typically 2,300 miles (3700km) (E and variants, 2,600 miles (4184km).

Armament: (All versions except EF, RF, QF which have no armament) four AIM-7 Sparrow air-to-air missiles recessed under fuselage; inner wing pylons can carry two more AIM-7 or four AIM-9 Sidewinder missiles; in

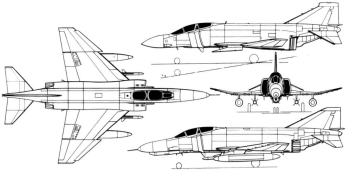

Three-view of F-4E, with (top) side view of F-4M.

addition all E versions except RF have internal 20mm M-61 multi-barrel gun, and virtually all versions can carry the same gun in external centreline pod; all except RF, QF have centreline and four wing pylons for tanks, bombs or other stores to total weight of 16,000lb (7257kg).

History: First flight (XF4H-1) 27 May 1958; service delivery (F-4A) February 1960 (carrier trials), February 1961 (inventory); first flight (Air Force F-4C) 27 May 1963; (YF-4K) 27 June 1966; (F-4E) 30 June 1967; (EF-4E) 1976.

Users: W Germany, Greece, Iran, Israel, Japan, Saudi Arabia, Singapore (no contract announced), S Korea, Spain, Turkey, UK (RAF, Royal Navy), USA (Air Force, ANG, Navy, Marine Corps).

Development: McDonnell designed the greatest fighter of the postwar era as a company venture to meet anticipated future needs. Planned as an attack aircraft with four 20mm guns, it was changed into a very advanced gunless all-weather interceptor with advanced radar and missile armament. In this form it entered service as the F-4A, soon followed by the F-4B used ▶

Left: An F-4B (since remanufactured as an F-4N) serving with US Navy fighter squadron VF-84 'Skull and Crossbones' aboard USS *Independence* during the Vietnam conflict.

Below left: The only Phantom IIs not built at St Louis were the 127 F-4EJ series assembled in Japan, mainly by Mitsubishi.

Below: This F-4E is equipped with the advanced AVQ-26 Pave Tack all-weather sighting and weapon-aiming system on a centreline pylon.

Above: In 1980 the Phantom II was still one of the most important tactical aircraft in the US inventory. This flight line full of F-4Ds could be at any of a dozen TAC or USAFE airbases; they are starting engines ready to move off on a training mission. This was the first purpose-designed version for operation from land bases. Some of this sub-type lack the prominent infra-red detector in the fairing under the radar.

in large numbers (635) by the US Navy and Marine Corps, with Westinghouse APQ-72 radar, IR detector in a small fairing under the nose, and many weapon options. Pilot and radar intercept officer sit in tandem and the aircraft has blown flaps and extremely comprehensive combat equipment. A level Mach number of 2·6 was achieved and many world records were set for speed, altitude and rate of climb. Not replaced by the abandoned F-111B, the carrier-based Phantom continued in production for 19 years through the F-4G with digital communications, F-4J with AWG-10 pulse-doppler radar, drooping ailerons, slatted tail and increased power, and the N (rebuilt B). In 1961 the F-4B was formally compared with all US Air Force fighters and found to outperform all by a wide margin, especially in weapon load and radar performance. As a result it was ordered in modified form as the F-110, soon redesignated F-4C, for 16 of the 23 Tactical Air Command Wings. The camera/radar/IR linescan RF-4C followed in 1965. In 1964 the Royal Navy adopted the Anglicised F-4K, with wider fuselage housing Spey fan engines and, of 48 delivered to Britain as Phantom FG.1, 28 served with the Royal

Navy. The other 20 went to RAF Strike Command, which has also received 120 F-4M (UK designation Phantom FGR.2) which combine the British features with those of the F-4C plus the option of a multi-sensor centreline reconnaissance pod whilst retaining full weapons capability. In the US Air Force the C was followed by the much-improved D with APQ-100 radar replaced by APQ-109, inertial navigation added and many added or improved equipment items. This in turn was followed by the dramatically improved F-4E with slatted wing, internal gun and increased power, the EJ being the version built in Japan and the F being a Luftwaffe version. The Luftwaffe also operate the multi-sensor RF-4E. Australia leased F-4Es from the US government pending delivery of the F-111C. In 1979 deliveries of new aircraft, all assembled at St Louis except for the EJ, were completed at 5,057, a record for any supersonic aircraft of any type in the Western world. In addition several large rebuild pro-grammes were in hand including rebuilding 300 F-4J into F-4S with long-life slatted airframes, rebuilding Marine Corps RF-4Bs with new structure and sensors, rebuilding or refitting over 600 Air Force machines (for example with Pave Tack FLIR/laser pods or Pave Spike TV/laser pods) and com-plete rebuild of 116 F-4D or E Phantoms into the EF-4E Wild Weasel defence-suppression platform with weapons replaced by special electronics (especially the APR-38 system, with large pod on the fin) to detect, locate and classify hostile electromagnetic emissions, and assist other aircraft to destroy them. Some EF aircraft may do their own killing, with Standard ARM, Shrike and Harm missiles.

McDonnell Douglas F-15 Eagle

F-15A, F-15B, F-15C, F-15D

Origin: McDonnell Aircraft, division of McDonnell Douglas Corp, St Louis, USA.

Type: Single-seat all-weather air-superiority fighter; (TF) dual-control trainer.

Engines: Two Pratt & Whitney F100-100 two-shaft augmented turbofans, each rated at 14,871lb (6744kg) thrust dry and 23,810lb (10,800kg) with maximum augmentation.

Dimensions: Span 42ft 9¾in (13·05m); length 63ft 9¾in (19·45m); height 18ft 7½in (5·68m).

Weights: Empty, about 28,000lb (12,700kg); loaded (F or TF, clean) 39,500lb; (F with four Sparrows) about 40,500lb, (three 600gal drop tanks) 54,000lb, (three tanks and two FAST packs) 66,000lb (29,937kg)

Performance: Maximum speed (low) over 921mph (1482km/h, Mach 1·22), (high) over 1,650mph (2660km/h, Mach 2·5); initial climb, over 50,000ft (15,240m)/min; service ceiling, over 70,000ft (21,000m); range on internal fuel, about 1,200 miles (1930km); ferry range with maximum fuel, over 3,700 miles (5955km).

Armament: One 20mm M-61 multi-barrel gun with 960 rounds; four AIM-7 Sparrow air-to-air missiles on corners of fuselage and four AIM-9 Sidewinder air-to-air missiles on lateral rails at upper level of wing pylons; centreline pylon stressed for 4,500lb (2041kg) for 600 gal tank, reconnaissance pod or any tactical weapon; inner wing pylons stressed for 5,100lb (2313kg) for any tanks or weapon; outer wing pylons stressed for 1,000lb (454kg) for ECM pods or equivalent ordnance load. Normal external load limit, with or without FAST packs, 12,000lb (5443kg).

History: First flight 27 July 1972; (TF) 7 July 1973; service delivery March 1974 (Cat. II test), November 1974 (inventory).

Users: Israel, Japan, Saudi Arabia, USA (Air Force).

Development: Emergence of the MiG-23 and -25 in 1967 accentuated the belief of the US Air Force that it was falling behind in true fighter aircraft. Studies for an FX (a new air-superiority fighter) were hastened and, after a ▶

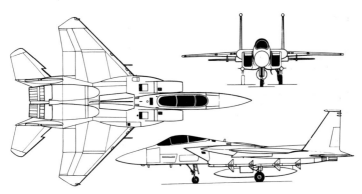

Above: Three-view of production F-15A Eagle.

Above: Examining the flat-plate antenna of the APG-63 radar.

Left: Landing gears begin to extend from an F-15A of the Heyl Ha'Avir (Israeli air force) carrying neither missiles nor tanks.

Below: Peel-off for landing by Eagles of the 1st Tactical Fighter Wing USAF at Langley AFB, Virginia (note TAC tail badges).

These USAF Eagles on detachment to an Arctic base were among the first to be seen with the painted radome which, after prolonged research, is now becoming standard. Low-visibility paint is now used over almost the entire aircraft, the problems with the radome including resistance to erosion by rain and hail, proper adhesion to a slightly flexible surface and avoidance of any degradation of radar performance. It is probable that similar coatings will become standard on other interceptors including RAF Phantoms.

major competition, McDonnell's team at St Louis was selected to build the new aircraft. The Air Force funded a new engine, won by Pratt & Whitney, and a new 25mm gun using caseless ammunition (abandoned after difficult development). The Eagle has emerged as probably the best fighter in the world, with thrust at low levels considerably greater than clean gross weight, a fixed wing of no less than 530 sq ft area, a single seat and an advanced Hughes X-band pulse-doppler radar. Though planned as an uncompromised machine for interception and air combat the Eagle also has formidable attack capability over intercontinental ranges. Undoubtedly its chief attributes are its combat manoeuvrability (it can outfly almost any other US machine without using afterburner) and the advanced automaticity of its radar, head-up display, weapon selectors and quick-fire capability. Internal fuel capacity of 11,200lb can be almost trebled by adding a FAST (fuel and sensor, tactical) pack on each side, a "conformal pallet" housing 10,000lb of fuel and target designators or weapons. Very extensive electronic systems for attack and defence, far beyond any standard previously seen in a fighter, are carried. A total USAF buy of 729 aircraft is planned, and though this has not changed since early in the programme the benefits of the "learning curve" (which reduces costs as production continues) are being much more than nullified by cost-inflation. The unit price of $7·5 million of 1975 had been more than doubled by late 1976 to over $16·7 million, with a figure in excess of $18 million predicted by Congress. Thus the 729 aircraft will now cost at least $12·2 billion, a figure rising by $500–700m each quarter. Nevertheless the outstanding qualities of this superbly capable fighter commend it to many governments; Israel has bought 21 new Eagles plus four reworked development aircraft, costing with support $600 million, and in mid-1976 the F-15 was chosen by Japan as the FX for the Air Self-Defence Force. The F-15B is a dual trainer, and the F-15C and D have increased internal fuel, FAST packs and new programmable radars with much-augmented capability.

Above: Two F-15As of the USAF Tactical Air Command on a ferry mission with centreline but no wing drop tanks.

Below left: An F-15A of the 1st TFW at Langley; other USAF units include the 57th (Nellis), 58th (Luke), 36th (Bitburg), 49th (Holloman), 33rd (Eglin) and 32nd TFS at Soersterburg.

Above: Start of a training sortie at a TAC base in the USA. Before takeoff the pilot will pivot the engine inlets downwards as seen in the photograph at left to match their shape to the angle of attack.

McDonnell Douglas F-101 Voodoo

F-101A, B and C and RF-101A to H

Origin: McDonnell Aircraft Co (division of McDonnell Douglas Corp), USA.
Type: (A, C) day fighter-bomber; (B) all-weather interceptor; (RF) all-weather reconnaissance.
Engines: Two Pratt & Whitney J57 two-shaft turbojets with afterburner; (F-101B) 14,990lb (6800kg) J57-53 or -55 (others) 14,880lb (6750kg) J57-13.
Dimensions: Span 39ft 8in (12·09m); length 67ft 4¾in (20·55m); (RF) 69ft 3in; height 18ft (5·49m).
Weights: Empty (typical of all) 28,000lb (12,700kg); maximum loaded (B) 46,700lb (21,180kg); (all versions, overload 51,000lb, 23,133kg).
Performance: Maximum speed (B) 1,220mph (1963km/h, Mach 1·85); (others, typical) 1,100mph; initial climb (B) 17,000ft (5180m)/min; service ceiling 52,000ft (15,850m); range on internal fuel (B) 1,550 miles (2500km); (others) 1,700 miles (2736km).
Armament: (B) three Falcon (usually AIM-4D) air-to-air missiles semi-submerged in underside, sometimes supplemented by two AIR-2A Genie nuclear rockets on fuselage pylons; (C) three 20mm M-39 cannon (provision for four, with Tacan removed) in fuselage; (RF) none. As built, all A and C and derivatives fitted with centreline crutch for 1 MT tactical nuclear store and wing pylons for two 2,000lb (907kg) bombs, four 680lb (310kg) mines or other ordnance.
History: First flight 29 September 1954; service delivery (A) May 1957; final delivery (B) March 1961.
Users: Canada, Taiwan, USA (ANG).

Development: By far the most powerful fighter of its day, the Voodoo was based on the XF-88 Voodoo prototype flown on 20 October 1948. Originally a long-range escort for Strategic Air Command, the F-101A became a tactical attack machine; 50 were followed by 47 improved C models, all of which set records for accident-free operation and were converted to unarmed RF-101G and H for the Air National Guard, augmenting

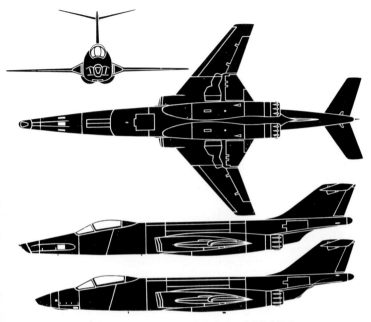

Above: RF-101C with (bottom) side view of RF-101G.

35 RF-101A and 166 RF-101C built earlier and used intensively at all levels in Vietnam. The B interceptor sacrificed fuel for a radar operator to work the MG-13 radar fire-control; 478 were built and converted to F-101F or dual-control TF-101F for Air Defense Command (now Air National Guard). In 1961 66 ex-ADC aircraft were transferred to the RCAF as CF-101s; in 1970 the CAF exchanged the 58 survivors for 66 improved F and TF and they still serve as the only CAF all-weather fighters.

Left: One of the rebuilds, an RF-101H. By 1980 the last G and H versions were being withdrawn from the ANG.

Left: A daytime recovery at a SE Asia base during the Vietnam war, in which the RF-101C (illustrated) was even more important than its successor, the RF-4C from the same manufacturer. CF-101s continue in service.

McDonnell Douglas/Hawker AV-8B

AV-8B and proposed variants

Origin: McDonnell Douglas Corporation (MCAIR, St Louis), USA; principal associate, British Aerospace (Hawker Aircraft, Kingston), UK.
Type: V/STOL light attack; proposed versions include sea-based air defence, reconnaissance and dual trainer/multi-role.
Engine: One Rolls-Royce Pegasus 103, (Pratt & Whitney F402) vectored-thrust turbofan rated at 21,500lb (9752kg).
Dimensions: Span 30ft 3½in (9·20m); length 42ft 11in (13·1m); height 11ft 3½in (3·4m).
Weights: Empty 12,400lb (5625kg); design, 22,750lb (10,320kg); loaded (close-support seven Mk 82 bombs) 25,994lb (11,790kg); maximum over 29,000lb (13,150kg).
Performance: Maximum speed, clean, over Mach 1; operational radius (VTO, 7,800lb/3538kg weapons) 115 miles (185km), (STO, 12 Mk 82 Snakeye, internal fuel) 172 miles (278km), (STO, seven Mk 82, external fuel) 748 miles (1204km); ferry range over 3,000 miles 4830km).
Armament: Two 20mm Mk 12 cannon in single belly pods, six underwing pylons and centreline hardpoint for weapon/ECM/fuel load of 8,000lb (3630kg) for VTO or 9,000lb (4080kg) for STO.
History: First flight (YAV-8B) 9 November 1978; operational capability originally planned for 1981–2.
Users: US Marine Corps, US Navy.

Development: Following proposals in 1973 by Hawker Siddeley and McDonnell Douglas for an advanced development of the Harrier the then UK Defence Minister, Roy Mason, said there was "not enough common ground" for a joint programme. This caused a delay of many months, but the US government eventually studied an improved aircraft designated AV-16A with a new wing and the uprated Pegasus 15 engine, before deciding to try to achieve as much as possible of the same advantages in payload/range and weapon load with the existing engine. Rolls-Royce and Pratt & Whitney have studied the Pegasus 11D (800lb extra thrust) and 11+ (1,000lb more) but these remained mere proposals as this book went to press, despite the fact Rolls-Royce ran a Pegasus at over 25,000lb thrust in May 1972. Under the present programme all changes are confined to the airframe, the main improvement being a completely new wing, with greater

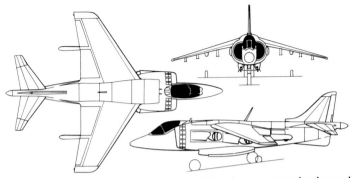

Above: Three-view of AV-8B Advanced Harrier as currently planned.

span and area, less sweep, a supercritical section and graphite-epoxy construction throughout the main wing box and large single-slotted flaps and drooping ailerons. Strakes and a large hinged belly flap will increase air pressure under the fuselage in VTO, while other changes include inlets matched to the engine (they are too small on previous production Harriers) and front nozzles cut off square with the efflux.

Overall improvement in payload/range, compared with an AV-8A, is about 100 per cent. There is still a chance that further gains may result from improvement to the F402 engine, and production AV-8Bs may have the raised cockpit of the British Sea Harrier. The US Marine Corps requirement is for 336, and a variant might possibly be purchased by the US Navy for its own use. Present plans envisage the AV-8B having the Angle-Rate Bombing System, with dual-mode TV and laser spot coupled via IBM computer to the Marconi-Elliott HUD. Fixed or retractable probe refuelling is likely, but radar will not be fitted. Two AV-8As were rebuilt by McDonnell Douglas as YAV-8Bs, and have performed very well in Navy/Marine Corps trials, but Congress has consistently shown itself hostile to what it regards as a foreign aircraft and production funds had been withheld as this book went to press despite sustained pleas from the Marines. The Navy has been more muted, but also wants a radar-equipped version known as AV-8B-Plus. If Congress should release funds, production aircraft would have about half British content, but would be assembled at St Louis.

Below: The first of two YAV-8B trials aircraft (rebuilt from AV-8As), hovering at the McDonnell Douglas plant at St Louis after 9 November 1978, which was when this important prototype first got its wheels off the ground.

McDonnell Douglas/Northrop F-18 Hornet and Cobra

F-18, TF-18 and F-18L

Origin: Original basic design, Northrop Corp; prime contractor, McDonnell Douglas Corp, USA, with Northrop building centre and aft fuselage.

Type: (F) single-seat carrier-based multi-role fighter, (TF) dual trainer, (A) single-seat land-based attack fighter.

Engines: Two 16,000lb (7257kg) thrust General Electric F404-400 two-shaft augmented turbofans.

Dimensions: Span (with missiles) 40ft 8½in (12·41m), (without missiles) 37ft 6in (11·42m); length 56ft (17·07m); height 14ft 9½in (4·50m).

Weights: (Provisional) empty 20,583lb (9336kg); loaded (clean) 33,642lb (15,260kg); maximum loaded (catapult limit) 50,064lb (22,710kg).

Performance: Maximum speed (clean, at altitude) 1,190mph (1915km/h, Mach 1·8), (maximum weight, sea level) subsonic; sustained combat manoeuvre ceiling, over 49,000ft (14,935m); absolute ceiling, over 60,000ft (18,290m); combat radius (air-to-air mission, high, no external fuel) 461 miles (741km); ferry range, not less than 2,300 miles (3700km).

Armament: One 20mm M61 Gatling in upper part of forward fuselage; nine external weapon stations for maximum load (catapult launch) of 13,400lb (6080kg), including bombs, sensor pods, ECM, missiles (including Sparrow) and other stores, with tip-mounted Sidewinders.

History: First flight (YF-17) 9 June 1974; (first of 11 test F-18) 18 November 1978; (production F-18) probably late 1980; service entry, planned for 1982.

User: USA (Navy, Marine Corps).

Development: In 1971 the US Navy became concerned at the cost of the F-14 and the resulting reduced rate of procurement and total number that could be afforded. In 1973 it studied low-cost versions and compared them with navalised F-15 versions and improved F-4s. In 1974 the VFX specification emerged for a wholly new and smaller fighter somewhat along the lines of the Air Force Air Combat Fighter. In May 1975 the Navy and Marine Corps announced their choice of the F-18, developed from the existing land-based Northrop F-17 by McDonnell Douglas and Northrop. In fact the F-18 will be almost twice as heavy as the original F-17 proposal but, with more powerful engines, is expected to have adequate dogfight performance through the 1980s. Features include an unswept wing with large dogteeth and forebody strakes at the roots, twin canted vertical tails, simple

Below: Takeoff by the first YF-18 Hornet prototype on 18 November 1978. All 11 flight-test aircraft had flown by 1980 and both land-based and early carrier trials were said to be promising.

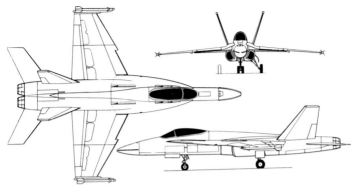

Above: Three-view of F-18 Hornet.

fixed engine inlets and extensive graphite/epoxy structure. Search radar will be used in the interception and surface-attack roles, and a very wide range of weapons will be carried. In the Navy air-superiority mission the gun will be backed up by two Sparrows and two Sidewinders, and the F-18 is expected to show dramatic improvements over the F-4J in manoeuvrability, reliability and low cost. In Marine attack missions the maximum load can be 14,000lb for airfield operation, and the inertial guidance and weapon-aiming are expected to offer a significant advance over the accuracy of any A-7. The Navy/Marines plan to buy 11 development aircraft plus 1,366 production machines during the 1980s, the original target price being about $5·9 million in 1975 dollars. Originally the Marine Corps version was to be designated A-18, because of its different mission equipment but it was later decided not to produce a dedicated attack version. Instead the Marine F-18 will replace the two Sparrow (or AMRAAM) missiles by a laser spot-tracker on one pylon and a forward-looking infra-red pod on the other. About one aircraft in every 13 will be a dual-control TF-18, with less internal fuel and no head-up display. In addition an RF-18 version has been proposed as a Fleet reconnaissance machine to replace the RF-8G and RA-5C, with a nose basically similar to that of the RF-5E.

In late 1976 Northrop — original designer of the YF-17 but a mere sub-contractor on the F-18 — was trying to relaunch the land-based Cobra, but now as a modified F-18. Despite severe competition from the F-16 and other aircraft, Northrop aims to find worldwide sales for the Cobra replacing the F-4, F-104, A-7 and Mirage. It would have less internal fuel than the F-18, and thus even higher performance. Planned export delivery date is 1983, priced at $8 million in 1975 dollars. This simplified land-based machine is designated F-18L, and is not normally named Hornet. Northrop is prime contractor for this project, which in late 1979 was being considered by Australia, Canada, Israel and Turkey, among other possible customers.

Mikoyan/Gurevich MiG-17

MiG-17, -17P, -17F (Lim-5P and -5M, S-104, F-4), -17PF and -17PFU (NATO name "Fresco")

Origin: The design bureau of Mikoyan and Gurevich, Soviet Union; licence-production as described in the text.

Type: Single-seat fighter; (PF, PFU) limited all-weather interceptor.

Engine: (-17, -17P) one 5,952lb (2700kg) thrust Klimov VK-1 single-shaft centrifugal turbojet; (later versions) one 4,732/7,452lb (3380kg) VK-1F with afterburner.

Dimensions: Span 31ft (9·45m); length (all) 36ft 3in (11·05m); height 11ft (3·35m).

Weights: Empty (all) about 9,040lb (4100kg); loaded (F, clean) 11,773lb (5340kg); maximum (all) 14,770lb (6700kg)

Performance: Maximum speed (F, clean at best height of 9,840ft) 711mph (1145km/h); initial climb 12,795ft (3900m)/min; service ceiling 54,460ft (16,600m); range (high, two drop tanks) 913 miles (1470km).

Armament: (-17) as MiG-15, one 37mm and two 23mm NS-23; (all later versions) three 23mm Nudelmann-Rikter NR-23 cannon, one under right side of nose and two under left; four wing hardpoints for tanks, total of 1,102lb (500kg) of bombs, packs of eight 55mm air-to-air rockets or various air-to-ground missiles.

History: First flight (prototype) January 1950; service delivery, 1952; service delivery (F-4) January 1956; final delivery (Soviet Union) probably 1959.

Users: Afghanistan, Albania, Algeria, Angola, Bulgaria, China, Cuba, Czechoslovakia, Egypt, E Germany, Guinea, Hungary, Indonesia (in storage), Iraq, Kampuchea, N Korea, Mali, Morocco (in storage), Nigeria, Poland, Romania, Somalia, S Yemen, Soviet Union, Sri Lanka, Sudan, Syria, Tanzania, Uganda, Vietnam, Yemen Arab.

Development: Only gradually did Western observers recognise the MiG-17 as not merely a slightly modified MiG-15 but a completely different aircraft. Even then it was generally believed it had been hastily designed to rectify deficiencies shown in the MiG-15's performance in Korea, but in fact the design began in about January 1949, long before the Korean war. This was because from the first the MiG-15 had shown bad behaviour at high speeds, and though the earlier fighter was eventually made completely safe (partly by arranging for the air brakes to open automatically at Mach 0·92) it was still a difficult gun platform due to its tendency to snake and pitch. The MiG-17 — which was probably the last fighter in which Gurevich played a direct personal role — had a new wing with thickness reduced from 11 per cent to about 9 per cent, a different section and planform and no fewer than

94

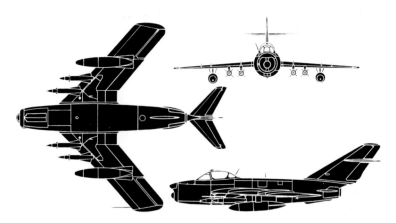

Above: Three-view of typical MiG-17F (NATO name, "Fresco C").

three fences. Without taper and with inboard sweep of 47° this made a big difference to high-Mach behaviour, and in fact there are reasons to believe the MiG-17 can be dived to make a sonic bang. With a new tail on a longer rear fuselage the transformation was completed by considerable revision of systems and equipment, though at first the VK-1 engine was unchanged. In 1958 the first limited all-weather version, the -17P, went into modest production with longer nose housing the same Izumrud ("Scan Odd") AI radar and ranging avionics as was also in production for the MiG-19. With the introduction of an afterburning engine the airbrakes were moved aft of the wing, away from the hot back end, but this was not a good position and they were returned (in enlarged rectangular form) to the tail in the most important sub-type the -17F. This was made in Poland as the Lim-5P (the -5M being a rough-field close-support version with larger tyres and drag chute), in Czechoslovakia as the S-104 and in China as the F-4. The PF was the afterburning all-weather version, and the final model was the PFU with guns removed and wing pylons for four beam-riding "Alkali" air-to-air missiles. Total production for at least 22 air forces must have considerably exceeded 5,000, exports from China alone exceeding 1,000. Many 17F remained in use in the mid-1970s.

Left: This MiG-17F is one of about 50 which in 1980 were still serving with the Syrian Air Force. Used in the low-level attack role, it is now obsolescent but may continue as a weapon trainer.

Below: Large numbers of many versions of MiG-17 remain in service with the air force of the Chinese People's Liberation Army, all with F-4 type designations. These appear to be normal F-4 fighter-bombers but at far right is a Chinese-developed TF-4 dual trainer.

Mikoyan/Gurevich MiG-19

MiG-19, -19S, -19SF (Lim-7, S-105, F-6), -19PF and -19PM; NATO name "Farmer"

Origin: The design bureau named for Mikoyan and Gurevich, Soviet Union; licence-production as described in the text.

Type: Single-seat fighter (PF, PM, all-weather interceptor).

Engines: (-19, -19S) two 6,700lb (3,040kg) thrust (afterburner rating) Mikulin AM-5 single-shaft afterburning turbojets; (-19SF, PF, PM) two 7,165lb (3250kg) thrust (afterburner) Klimov RD-9B afterburning turbojets.

Dimensions: Span 29ft 6½in (9m); length (S, SF, excluding pitot boom) 42ft 11¼in (13·08m); (-19PF, PM) 44ft 7in; height 13ft 2¼in (4·02m).

Weights: Empty (SF) 12,698lb (5760kg); loaded (SF, clean) 16,755lb (7600kg); (maximum, SF) 19,180lb (8700kg); (PM) 20,944lb (9500kg).

Performance: Maximum speed (typical) 920mph at 20,000ft (1480km/h, Mach 1·3); initial climb (SF) 22,640ft (6900m)/min; service ceiling (SF) 58,725ft (17,900m); maximum range (high, with two drop tanks) 1,367 miles (2200km).

Armament: See text.

History: First flight, September 1953; service delivery early 1955; first flight (F-6) December 1961.

Users: Afghanistan, Albania, Bulgaria, China, Cuba, Czechoslovakia, E Germany (not operational), Hungary, Indonesia (in storage), Iraq, N Korea, Pakistan, Poland, Romania, Soviet Union, Tanzania (F6), Vietnam, Zambia (F6).

Development: With the MiG-19 the Mikoyan-Gurevich bureau established itself right in the front rank of the world's fighter design teams. The new fighter was on the drawing board as the I-350 before even the MiG-15 had been encountered in Korea, the five prototypes being ordered on 30 July 1951. Maj. Grigori Sedov flew the first aircraft on 18 September 1953 on the power of two non-afterburning AM-5 engines giving only 4,410lb thrust each. Nevertheless, despite the high wing loading and bold sweep angle of 55° (at 25% chord), the MiG-19 handled well, large fences and Fowler flaps giving satisfactory low-speed control. With afterburning engines the MiG-19 became the first Russian supersonic fighter and it was put into production on a very large scale, rivalling that of the MiG-15 and -17, despite a 100 per cent increase in price. After about 500 had been delivered the MiG-19S (*stabilizator*) supplanted the early model with the fixed tail-plane and manual elevators replaced by a fully powered slab. At the same time the old armament (unchanged since MiG-15 and -17) was replaced by three of the new 30mm NR-30 guns, one in each wing root and one under the right side of the nose. A large ventral airbrake was also added. In 1956 the AM-5 engine was replaced by the newer and more powerful RD-9,

Right: Few of this specialized missile-armed interceptor version (the MiG-19PM, which unlike earlier MiG fighters was not made in Poland) remain in service with the PWL (Polish Air Force).

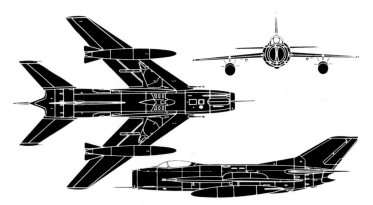

Above: Three-view of MiG-19SF (Shenyang F-6).

increasing peak Mach number from 1·1 to 1·3. The new fighter was designated MiG-19SF (*forsirovanni*, increased power), and has been built in very large numbers. Total production possibly exceeds 10,000, including licence-manufacture as the Lim-7 in Poland, S-105 in Czechoslovakia and F-6 in China. The corresponding MiG-19PF (*perekhvatchik*, interceptor) has an Izumrud AI radar (called "Scan Odd" by NATO) in a bullet carried on the inlet duct splitter, with the ranging unit in the upper inlet lip, changing the nose shape and adding 22in to the aircraft length. The final production version was the MiG-19PM (*modifikatsirovanni*), with guns removed and pylons for four early beam-rider air-to-air missiles (called "Alkali" by NATO). All MiG-19s can carry the simple K-13A missile (the copy of Sidewinder, called "Atoll" by NATO) and underwing pylons can carry two 176 gal drop tanks plus two 551lb weapons or dispensers. Perhaps surprisingly, there has been no evidence of a two-seat trainer version of this fine fighter, which in 1960 was judged obsolescent and in 1970 was fast being reappraised as an extremely potent dogfighter. Part of the understanding of the MiG-19's qualities has resulted from its purchase in large numbers by Pakistan as the F-6 from the Chinese factory at Shenyang. The notable features of the F-6 were its superb finish, outstanding dogfight manoeuvrability and tremendous hitting power of the NR-30 guns, each projectile having more than twice the kinetic energy of those of the Aden or DEFA of similar calibre. Though China soon ceased making the MiG-21 the F-6 remains in production, and has been developed into the F-6bis.

Left: Very large numbers of many versions of F-6 (Chinese-built MiG-19) are used by the air force of the Chinese People's Liberation Army. This is a regular F-6 single-seat tactical machine, but some versions — notably the TF-6 dual-control trainer — are wholly of Chinese design and have no counterpart in the Soviet Union. The F-6 was also the basis for the much heavier and more powerful F-6bis, called 'Fantan-A' by NATO.

Mikoyan/Gurevich MiG-21

MiG-21, 21F (S-107), 21FA, 21PF, 21FL, 21PFS, 21PFM, 21PFMA, 21M, 21R, 21MF, 21SMT, 21bis, 21U, 21US and 21UM plus countless special versions. Several versions made in China as F-8

Origin: The design bureau named for Mikoyan and Gurevich; Soviet Union; licence-production as described in the text.

Type: Single-seat fighter; (PFMA and MF) limited all-weather multi-role; (R) reconnaissance; (U) two-seat trainer.

Engine: In all versions, one Tumansky single-shaft turbojet with afterburner; (-21) R-11 rated at 11,240lb (5100kg) with afterburner; (-21F) R-11-F2-300 rated at 13,120lb (5950kg); (-21FL, PFS, PFM and PFMA) R-11-G2S-300 rated at 13,668lb (6200kg); (-21MF and derivatives) R-13-300 rated at 14,500lb (6600kg).

Dimensions: Span 23ft 5½in (7.15m); length (excluding probe) (-21) 46ft 11in; (-21MF) 48ft 0½in (14.6m); height (little variation, but figure for MF) 14ft 9in (4.5m).

Weights: Empty (-21) 11,464lb (5200kg); (-21MF) 12,346lb (5600kg); maximum loaded (-21) 18,740lb (8500kg); (-21MF) 21,605lb (9800kg) (weight with three tanks and two K-13A, 20,725lb).

Performance: Maximum speed (MF, but typical of all) 1,285mph (2070km/h, Mach 2.1); initial climb (MF, clean) 36,090ft (11,000m)/min; service ceiling 59,050ft (18,000m); range (high, internal fuel) 683 miles (1100km); maximum range (MF, high, three tanks) 1,118 miles (1800km).

Armament: See text.

Above: One of the intermediate versions, a MiG-21MF (in Egyptian AF service).

Right: An early model, MiG-21FL, on night-flying practice with the East German (LSK) air force. This sub-type is not equipped for night fighting, though with good ground guidance it might get into a firing position.

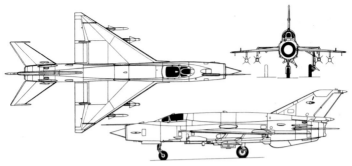

Above: Three-view of MiG-21SMT ("Fishbed K") with four K-13A missiles.

History: First flight (E-5 prototype) late 1955; (production -21F) late 1957; service delivery early 1958.

Users: Afghanistan, Albania, Algeria, Angola, Bangladesh, Bulgaria, China, Cuba, Czechoslovakia, Egypt, Ethiopia, Finland, E Germany, Hungary, India (licence-built), Indonesia (stored), Iraq, Laos, Mozambique, Nigeria, N Korea, Poland, Romania, Somalia, Soviet Union, Sudan, S Yemen, Syria, Tanzania, Uganda, Vietnam, Yemen Arab Republic, Yugoslavia.

Development: Undoubtedly the most widely used combat aircraft in the world in the 1970s, this trim little delta has destabled a reputation for cost effectiveness and in its later versions it also packs a more adequate ▶

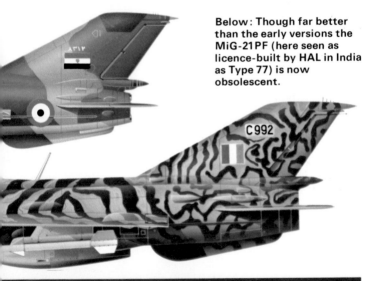

Below: Though far better than the early versions the MiG-21PF (here seen as licence-built by HAL in India as Type 77) is now obsolescent.

multi-role punch. It was designed in the 18 months following the Korean War. While Sukhoi developed large supersonic fighters to rival the American F-100, the Mikoyan-Gurevich bureau, by now led only by Col-Gen Mikoyan (who died in 1970), concentrated on a small day interceptor of the highest possible performance. Prototypes were built with both swept and delta wings, both having powered slab tailplanes, and the delta was chosen for production. At least 30 pre-production aircraft had flown by the time service delivery started and the development effort was obviously considerable. The initial MiG-21 abounded in interesting features including Fowler flaps, fully powered controls, upward ejection seat fixed to the rear of the front-hinged canopy (which incorporated the whole front of the cockpit enclosure except the bullet-proof windshield) to act as a pilot blast-shield, and internal fuel capacity of only 410 gal. Armament was two 30mm NR-30 in long fairings under the fuselage, the left gun usually being replaced by avionics. Part of these avionics serve the two K-13 ("Atoll") missiles carried on wing pylons on the slightly more powerful 21F. This had radar ranging, 515 gal fuel, broader fin, upward-hinged pitot boom attached under the nose (to prevent people walking into it) and two dorsal blade aerials. Czech-built aircraft (still called 21F) did not have the rear-view windows in the front of the dorsal spine. The F was called "Fishbed C" by NATO and Type 74 by the Indian Air Force; it was also the type supplied to China in 1959 and used as the pattern for the Chinese-built F-8. As the oldest active variant it was also the first exported or seen in the West, the Finnish AF receiving the 21F-12 in April 1963.

At Tushino in 1961 the prototype was displayed of what became the 21PF, with inlet diameter increased from 27in to 36in, completely changing the nose shape and providing room for a large movable centre-body housing the scanner of the R1L (NATO "Spin Scan") AI radar. Other changes include deletion of guns (allowing simpler forward airbrakes), bigger main-wheels (causing large fuselage bulges above the wing), pitot boom moved above the inlet, fatter dorsal spine (partly responsible for fuel capacity of 627gal) and many electronic changes. All PF had an uprated engine, late models had take-off rocket latches and final batches had completely new

Above: Though the latest type of combat aircraft so far permitted to the air force of Romania is the very limited MiG-21PF, with 'AA-2 Atoll' IR-homing missiles, it is possible that an air-combat version of the Orao may appear. About 80 of all MiG-21 versions are believed to be in service with this country.

blown flaps (SPS) which cut landing speed by 25mph and reduced nose-up attitude for better pilot view. The FL was the export PF (L = *lokator*, denoting R2L radar) with even more powerful engine. Like the F models rebuilt in 1963-64, this can carry the GP-9 gunpack housing the excellent GSh-23 23mm twin-barrel gun, has a still further broadened vertical tail and drag-chute repositioned above the jetpipe. The PFS was the PF with SPS blown flaps, while the PFM was a definitive improved version with another 19in added to the fin (final fillet eliminated), a conventional seat and side-hinged canopy, and large flush aerials in the fin. One-off versions were built to prove STOL with lift jets and to fly a scaled "analogue" of the wing of the Tu-144 SST. The very important PFMA, made in huge numbers, was the first multi-role version, with straight top line from much deeper spine (housing equipment and not fuel and holding tankage to 572gal), and four pylons for two 1,100lb and two 551lb bombs, four S-24 missiles and/or tanks or K-13A missiles. The 21M has an internal GSh-23 and since 1973 has been built in India as Type 88. The 21R has multi-sensor reconnaissance internally and in pods and wing-tip ECM fairings, as do late models of the 21MF, the first to have the new R-13 engine. The RF is the R-13-powered reconnaissance version. One of the few variants still in production is the SMT, with fuel restored to the spine and more comprehensive avionics including tail-warning radar.

Code-named "Mongol" and called Type 66 in India, the U is the tandem trainer, the US has SPS flaps and UM the R-13 engine and four pylons. Many other versions have been used to set world records. About 10,000 of all sub-types have been built, and in 1977 output was continuing at perhaps three per week in the Soviet Union, with a much lower rate in India; in early 1976 N Korea was said to be also in production. Many of the early models of this neat fighter were sweet to handle and quite effective day dogfighters, but the majority of the subtypes in use have many adverse characteristics and severe limitations.

In late 1976 a new version appeared, the MiG-21bis (Fishbed L); this is a cleaned-up and refined MiG-21MF with Tacan-type navigation and other improvements.

Below: A fine picture of a MiG-21bis, which (depending on whether the engine is the R-13-300 or the more powerful R-25) has the NATO code-name 'Fishbed-L' or 'Fishbed-N'. Many other variants are broadly similar.

Mikoyan/Gurevich MiG-23

MiG-23, -23S and -23U ("Flogger")

Origin: The design bureau named for Mikoyan and Gurevich, Soviet Union; no production outside the Soviet Union yet reported.

Type: (-23S, Flogger B) single-seat all-weather interceptor with Flogger E export variant of unknown designation; (-23U, Flogger C) dual-control trainer and ECM platform.

Engine: One Tumansky afterburning turbofan, believed to be an R-29B rated at 17,640lb (8000kg) dry and 25,350lb (11,500kg) with afterburner.

Dimensions: (Estimated) Span (72° sweep) 28ft 7in (8·7m), (16°) 47ft 3in (14·4m); length (export) 53ft (16·15m), (S, U) 55ft 1½in (16·80m); height 13ft (3·96m).

Weights: (Estimated) empty 17,500lb (7940kg); loaded (clean or fighter mission) 30,000lb (13,600kg); maximum permissible 33,000lb (15,000kg).

Performance: Maximum speed, clean, 840mph (1350km/h, Mach 1·1) at sea level; maximum speed with missiles, at altitude, 1,520mph (2445km/h, Mach 2·3); service ceiling about 61,000ft (18,600m); combat radius (hi-lo-hi) about 600 miles (966km).

Armament: (-23S) one 23mm GSh-23 twin-barrel gun on ventral centreline, plus various mixes of air/air missiles which usually include one or two infra-red or radar-homing AA-7 "Apex" and/or infra-red or radar-homing AA-8 "Aphid", the latter for close combat; (-23U) none reported.

History: First flight, probably 1965; (first production aircraft) believed 1970; service delivery, believed 1971.

Users: Algeria, Bulgaria, Czechoslovakia, Egypt, Ethiopia, East Germany, Iraq, Libya, Poland, Soviet Union, Syria.

continued ▶

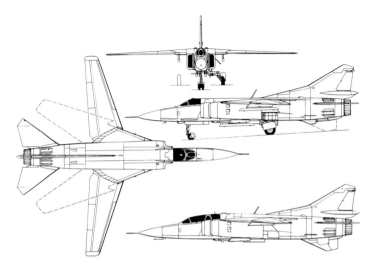

Above: Three-view of MiG-23S, with side view of MiG-23U trainer (lower right).

Left: A MiG-23S or 'Flogger-B' air-combat fighter of the Soviet air force, probably from an IA-PVO air-defence unit.

Below: Night training by PVO unit equipped with MiG-23S. This example, with missile pylons tantalisingly empty, is taxiing with wings swept, which may be standard procedure with such aircraft.

Development: Revealed at the 1967 Moscow Aviation Day, the prototype swing-wing MiG-23 was at first thought to be a Yakovlev design, though it appeared in company with a jet-lift STOL fighter having an identical rear fuselage and tail and strong MiG-21-like features (though much bigger than a MiG-21). Over the next four years the Mikoyan bureau greatly developed this aircraft, which originally owed something to the F-111 and Mirage G. By 1971 the radically different production versions, the -23S fighter and -23U trainer, were entering service in quantity, and by 1975 several hundred had been delivered to Warsaw Pact air forces and also to Egypt. Today Egypt is believed no longer to operate the type, but large deliveries have been made to other countries. The MiG-27 attack version is described separately.

There are three main versions. The first to enter service was the MiG-23S all-weather interceptor, with powerful highly-afterburning engine, "High Lark" nose radar (said in 1973 by the then Secretary of the USAF to be "comparable with that of the latest Phantom") and, almost certainly, a

Above: Called 'Flogger-E' by NATO. this specially simplified version of MiG-23 is the only one cleared for export. This example is one of 50 serving at El Adem with the Libyan Republic Air Force, and photographed by a passenger in a Western airliner. Very similar aircraft in service with the Soviet Union created an excellent impression on a visit to Finland in 1978. They carried no missiles, laser or doppler.

Right: Taken from a Soviet film, this unusual view of a MiG-23S again shows that it is apparently normal to have the wings swept on the ground. According to the US Department of Defense this 'Flogger-B' version is the first Russian aircraft "with a demonstrated capability to track and engage targets flying below its own altitude". About 1,000 were in PVO service by 1980.

laser ranger and doppler navigator. ECM and other EW equipment is markedly superior to anything fitted in previous Soviet aircraft, and apparently as good as comparable installations in Western fighters (other than the F-15).

Several hundred S models are in service with the IA-PVO and Warsaw Pact air forces, and they are replacing the Su-9 and -11 and Yak-28P. Missiles are carried on a centreline pylon (which often carries a drop-tank instead), on pylons under the inlet ducts and under the fixed wing gloves (centre section). For overseas customers a simplified sub-type is in production, with the same high-Mach airframe and systems as the -23S fighter but lacking the latter's radar (NATO calls this model "Flogger E" but the Soviet designation was unknown as this book went to press). The third MiG-23 so far seen is the tandem two-seat -23U, used for conversion training and as an ECM and reconnaissance platform. This again has the fighter's high-speed airframe and systems, but has not been seen with any weapons or delivery systems.

Mikoyan/Gurevich MiG-25

Mig-25 ("Foxbat A"), -25R and -25U

Origin: The design bureau named for Mikoyan and Gurevich, Soviet Union.
Type: "Foxbat A" (believed to be MiG-25S), all-weather long-range interceptor; MiG-25R, reconnaissance; MiG-25U, tandem-seat dual trainer with stepped cockpits.
Engines: Two Tumansky R-31 afterburning turbojets each rated at 27,000lb (12,250kg) with full augmentation.
Dimensions: Span 46ft (14·0m); length ("A") 73ft 2in (22·3m), (R) 74ft 6in (22·7m), (U) about 76ft (23·16m); height 18ft 6in (5·63m).
Weights: (Fighter) empty 44,000lb (19,960kg); normal loaded 68,350lb (31,000kg); maximum loaded with external missiles or tanks 79,800lb (36,200kg).
Performance: (Estimated) maximum speed at altitude 2,100mph (3380km/h, Mach 3·2); initial climb, about 50,000ft (15,240m)/min; service ceiling 73,000ft (22,250m); high-altitude combat radius without external fuel, 700 miles (1130km).
Armament: ("-A") four underwing pylons each carrying one AA-6 air-to-air missile (two radar, two infra-red) or other store; no guns; ("-B") none.
History: First flight (E-266 prototype) probably 1964; (production reconnaissance version) before 1969; (production interceptor) probably 1969; service delivery (both) 1970 or earlier.
Users: Algeria, Libya, Soviet Union.

Development: This large and powerful aircraft set a totally new level in combat-aircraft performance. The prototypes blazed a trail of world records in 1965–67 including closed-circuit speeds, payload-to-height and rate of climb records. The impact of what NATO quickly christened "Foxbat" was unprecedented. Especially in the Pentagon, Western policymakers recognised that here was a combat aircraft that outclassed everything else, and urgent studies were put in hand for a new US Air Force fighter (F-15 Eagle) to counter it. By 1971 at least two pairs of reconnaissance aircraft were flying with impunity over Israel, too high and fast for Phantoms to catch, while others have made overflights deep into Iran. This version is different in many respects, the nose having cameras instead of a "Fox Fire" radar, and other sensors being carried under the large body. Both versions have twin outward-sloping vertical tails, single mainwheels and a flush canopy

Above: Night
takeoff by a
section of MiG-
25 'Foxbat-A' all-
weather inter-
ceptors.

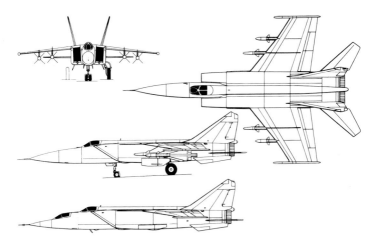

Above: Three-view of MiG-25 ("Foxbat A") with side view (bottom) of -25U.

shaped for speed rather than pilot view. From the start the main development effort has been applied to the basic MiG-25 (so-called "Foxbat A") interceptor, which has been developed in structure, systems and armament since first entering service with the PVO. In 1975 the original AA-5 missiles were supplemented, and later replaced, by the monster AA-6 "Acrid", which is easily the biggest air/air missile in service in the world. The radar-homing version has a length of about 20ft 2in (6·15m) and effective range of 28 miles (45km); the infra-red missiles have a length of just over 19ft (5·8m) and range of some 12·5 miles (20km). Another major improvement since entering service is flight-refuelling capability, not yet fitted to all MiG-25 versions. The detailed inspection of an interceptor version landed at Hakodate AB, Japan, on 6 September 1976, showed that in service pilots are forbidden to use the limits of the available flight performance, presumably to avoid thermal fatigue of the airframe; it also showed this particular machine to have early "Fox Fire" radar comparable in basic technology with the AWG-10 Phantom radar (as would be expected). Radars in current production are unquestionably solid-state pulse-doppler types able to look down and track low-flying aircraft against ground clutter. Several MiG-25s, most of them MiG-25R models on ELINT missions, have been plotted by Western radars at Mach 2·8. It should be emphasized that at this speed the MiG-25 — and any other aircraft — flies in a straight line. The MiG-25 was not designed for air combat, and if it became involved in a dogfight its speed would — like any other aircraft — soon be subsonic. The MiG-25U trainer carries neither weapons nor sensors, but is needed to convert pilots to what is still, 15 years after design, a very advanced and demanding aircraft.

Below: Artist's impression of the basic 'Foxbat-A' interceptor version of MiG-25, essentially similar to the aircraft in which Lt Belenko defected to Japan in 1976.

Mikoyan/Gurevich MiG-27

MiG-27 "Flogger D" and "Flogger F"

Origin: The design bureau named for Mikoyan and Gurevich, Soviet Union; no production outside the Soviet Union yet reported.

Type: Single-seat tactical attack, probably with reconnaissance capability.

Engine: One Tumansky R-29B afterburning turbofan rated at 17,640lb (8000kg) dry and 25,350lb (11,500kg) with full afterburner.

Dimensions: Similar to MiG-23 except fuselage nose is longer but pitot head shorter giving fractionally shorter overall length; height about 15ft (4·6m).

Weights (estimated): Empty 17,300lb (7850kg); maximum loaded 44,310lb (20,100kg).

Performance: Maximum speed at low level (clean) about Mach 1·0, (maximum weight) subsonic; maximum speed at high altitude (clean) about 1,055mph (1700km/h, Mach 1·6); take-off to 50ft (15m) at 34,600lb (15,700kg) 2,625ft (800m); service ceiling (clean) about 50,000ft (15,250m); combat radius with bombs and one tank (hi-lo-hi) 600 miles (960km); ferry range (wings spread with three tanks) over 2,000 miles (3200km).

Armament: One 23mm six-barrel Gatling-type gun in belly fairing; seven external pylons (centreline, fuselage flanks under inlet ducts, fixed wing gloves and swing-wings) for wide range of ordnance including guided missiles (AS-7 "Kerry") and tactical nuclear weapons to total weight of 4,200lb (1900kg). All ECM are internal and all pylons are thus usable by weapons or tanks. Those on the outer wings are not always fitted; they are piped for drop tanks, but do not pivot and thus may be loaded only when the wings remain unswept.

History: First flight, possibly about 1970; service delivery, before 1974.

Users: Cuba, Egypt, E Germany, Iraq, Poland, Soviet Union, Syria.

Development: Derived from the same variable-geometry prototype flown by the MiG bureau at the 1967 Aviation Day, this aircraft was at first called "MiG-23B" in the West but is now known to have a different Soviet service designation that is almost certainly MiG-27. Bureau numbers are generally unknown for the MiG series; Mikoyan himself died in December 1970 and Gurevich in November 1976, and recent designs are known only by their service numbers. Compared with the MiG-23 this attack version carries heavier loads and is simpler and optimised for low-level operation. The airframe differs in having a shallower nose with a flat pointed profile housing mapping/terrain-following radar, laser ranger, doppler radar and radio altimeter, with good pilot view ahead and downward. The cockpit is heavily armoured. The engine is more powerful than that of the MiG-23 but is fed by fixed inlets and has a shorter and simpler nozzle. Main wheels are fitted with large low-pressure tyres, and special provision is made for rough-field operation. Internal ECM equipment is extensive, and pods on the wing-glove leading edges appear to contain an opto-electronic seeker (left) and passive radar receiver (right). Internal fuel capacity is estimated at 1,183 Imp gallons

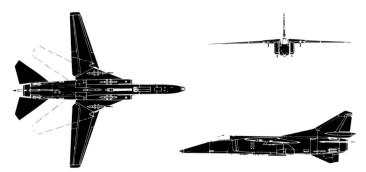

Above: Three-view of MiG-27 without swing-wing pylons.

(5380lit) including fuel in the fin; no provision for flight refuelling has been noted. The "Flogger F" has the engine installation and gun of the MiG-23, with variable inlets, and lack the comprehensive MiG-27 avionics. These are thought to be development aircraft or an export version. Possible problems with the basic aircraft are suggested by reports that in a few months the Syrian AF has written off 13 out of 50 supplied.

Above: Russian pilots pose for a propaganda picture in front of their extremely well-equipped MiG-27 'Flogger-D' attack aircraft.

Below: Egyptian 'Flogger-F' versions have export designation MiG-23.

Mitsubishi F-1 and T-2

F-1 and T-2A

Origin: Mitsubishi Heavy Industries Ltd, Japan.
Type: (T-2A) two-seat supersonic trainer; (F-1) single-seat close-support fighter-bomber.
Engines: Two Ishikawajima-Harima TF40-801A (licence-built Rolls-Royce/Turboméca Adour 102) two-shaft augmented turbofans with maximum rating of 7,140lb (3238kg); (F-1) may later have more powerful version.
Dimensions: Span 25ft 10in (7·87m); length 58ft 7in (17·86m); height (T-2) 14ft 7in (4·445m), (F-1) 14ft 9in.
Weights: Empty (T-2) 13,668lb (6200kg); (F-1) 14,330lb (6500kg); loaded (T-2, clean) 21,274lb (9650kg); (T-2 maximum) 24,750lb (11,200 kg); (F-1 maximum) 30,200lb (13,700kg).
Performance: Maximum speed (at clean gross weight) 1,056mph (1700km/h, Mach 1·6); initial climb 19,680ft (6000m)/min; service ceiling 50,025ft (15,250m); range (T-2 with external tanks) 1,785 miles (2870km); (F-1 with eight 500lb bombs) 700 miles (1126km).
Armament: One 20mm M-61 multi-barrel gun under left side of cockpit floor; pylon hardpoints under centreline and inboard and outboard on wings, with light stores attachments at tips. Total weapon load (T-2) normally

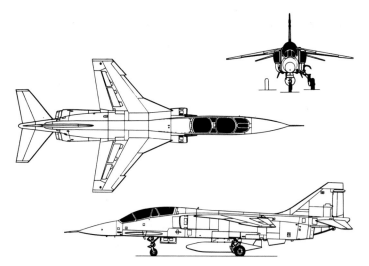

Three-view of Mitsubishi T-2A without wing pylons.

2,000lb (907kg); (F-1) 6,000lb (2722kg) comprising 12,500lb bombs, eight 500lb plus two tanks of 183gal, or two 1,300lb (590kg) ASM-1 anti-ship missiles, and four Sidewinders.

History: First flight (XT-2) 20 July 1971; (T-2A) January 1975; (FST-2) June 1975; service delivery (T-2A) March 1975; (F-1) 1977.

User: Japanese Air Self-Defence Force.

Development: Japan's first post-war military aircraft was the Fuji T-1 tandem-seat intermediate trainer, looking like an F-86 Sabre and powered by a licence-built Bristol Orpheus. First flown in 1958, 42 were delivered as the T-1A, followed by 22 T-1B with the Japanese J3 engine. To replace the T-1 and other trainers such as the T-33 a design team led by Dr Kenji Ikeda designed the T-2, Japan's first supersonic aircraft, using the Anglo-French Jaguar as a basis. After flight trials had shown the validity of the design a single-seat version, the FST-2-Kai, was ordered to replace the F-86 as a close-support fighter. By mid-1975 orders had been placed for 46 T-2A trainers and the first 4th Air Wing unit had formed at Matsushima Air Base. The T-2A has proved efficient and popular in service, and is incidentally the first properly supersonic aircraft to be designed in Asia. Though a trainer, it carries Mitsubishi Electric radar, with air search, mapping, lock-on and ranging modes, as well as a J/AWG-11 (Thomson-CSF) HUD. Production is at the rate of two per month; by the start of 1977 orders stood at the planned level of 59, to be completed in 1980, and deliveries at 37. The first 18 FST-2 fighters (since redesignated F-1) had also been bought, with four flown in 1975. Total F-1 procurement is to be 68, all delivered by the end of 1979. The F-1 has a Ferranti inertial nav/attack system and Mitsubishi Electric weapon-aiming computer, radar altimeter and radar homing and warning system, most of the added boxes being installed in the bay occupied by the rear cockpit in the T-2A. Production began in 1977, with the letter of intent for a force of 68, all to be delivered by March 1980. Planned total is 110.

Left: From this angle only an expert could tell that this is not an F-1 but a dual T-2A trainer, 71 of which are to be used at the 4th Air Wing base at Matsushima. Of these, 31 are of the basic T-2 type, while the other 40 are T-2A combat trainers with internal 'Gatling gun' and various other changes. A further two aircraft were converted into prototypes of the F-1 single-seat combat aircraft, 36 of which had been delivered by 1980.

North American (Rockwell) F-100 Super Sabre

F-100A to F-100F and DF-100F

Origin: North American Aviation Inc, Inglewood, USA.

Type: Single-seat fighter-bomber; (F-100F) two-seat operational trainer; (DF) missile or RPV director aircraft.

Engine: One Pratt & Whitney J57 two-shaft turbojet with afterburner, (most blocks of A) 14,500lb (6576kg) J57-7; (late A, all C) 16,000lb (7257kg) J57-29; (D, F) 16,950lb (7690kg) J57-21A (all ratings with afterburner).

Dimensions: Span (original A) 36ft 7in; (remainder) 38ft 9½in (11·81m); length (except F, excluding pitot boom) 49ft 6in (15·09m), (fuselage, 47ft exactly); (F) 52ft 6in (16·0m), (boom adds about 6ft to all models); height (original A) 13ft 4in; (remainder) 16ft 2¾in (4·96m).

Weights: Empty (original A) 19,700lb; (C) 20,450lb; (D) 21,000lb (9525kg); (F) 22,300lb (10,115kg); maximum loaded (original A) 28,935lb; (C, D) 34,832lb (15,800kg); (F, two tanks but no weapons) 30,700lb (13,925kg).

Performance: Maximum speed (typical of all) 864mph at height (1390 km/h, Mach 1·31); initial climb (clean) 16,000ft (4900m)/min; service ceiling (typical) 45,000ft (13,720m); range (high, two 375gal tanks) 1,500 miles (2415km).

Armament: Usually four (F, only two) 20mm M-39E cannon each with 200 rounds; (A) pylons for two 375gal supersonic tanks and four additional hardpoints (seldom used) for 4,000lb ordnance; (C, D) two tanks and six pylons for 7,500lb (3402kg) ordnance; (F) two tanks and maximum of 6,000lb (2722kg) ordnance.

History: First flight (YF-100) 25 May 1953; production (A) 29 October 1953; final delivery October 1959.

Users: Denmark, Taiwan, Turkey.

Development: The success of the Sabre made it natural to attempt a successor, and in February 1949 this was planned as a larger and much more powerful machine able to exceed the speed of sound in level flight (had it been started two years later it might have been smaller, in view of the Korean pressure for simple fighters with the highest possible climb and performance at extreme altitudes). Unusual features were the 6 per cent wing with 45° sweep, no flaps, inboard ailerons, full-span slats and a slab

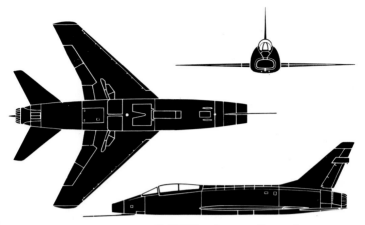

Three-view of tandem-seat F-100F in clean configuration.

tailplane mounted as low as possible. Level supersonic speed was achieved, for the first time with a combat aircraft, but after very rapid development, with the first (479th) wing fully equipped, the F-100A was grounded in November 1954. Trouble due to inertia coupling between the roll and yaw axes necessitated urgent modification, the wings and fin being lengthened. Subsequently the career of the "Hun" was wholly successful, the 203 A fighters being followed by the stronger C fighter-bomber, the D with flaps and autopilot and the tandem-seat F. Total production was lower than expected at 2,294, many being built by NAA's newly occupied factory at Columbus, Ohio. In their early years the later versions pioneered global deployment of tactical aircraft by means of probe/drogue refuelling, and in Vietnam they proved outstandingly good at both low attack and top cover, flying more missions than over 15,000 Mustangs flew in World War II. In 1977 the survivors of what two decades earlier had been among the world's élite warplanes were in their final months of combat duty after countless inspection, repair and modification programmes.

Left: Turkey is one of the last nations to retain a force of F-100 Super Sabres; this is an F-100D-15 single-seat ground-attack aircraft.

Below: At one time the USAF operated the GAM-83 (later restyled AGM-12) Bullpup command-guided air-to-surface missile from the F-100, though it was withdrawn before the aircraft itself (which remained in service after the war in Vietnam).

Northrop F-5 Freedom Fighter and Tiger II

F-5A, B, E and F, CF-5A and D, NF-5A and B, RF-5A, E and G, and SF-5A and B

Origin: Northrop Aircraft Division, Hawthorne, USA; made or assembled under licence by partnership Canada/Netherlands and by Spain.

Type: (With suffix A, E, and G) single-seat fighter-reconnaissance; (with suffix B, D and F) two-seat dual fighter/trainer.

Engines: (A, B, D, G) two 4,080lb (1850kg) thrust General Electric J85-13 single-shaft afterburning turbojets; (E, F) two 5,000lb (2268kg) J85-21.

Dimensions: Span (A, B, D, G) 25ft 3in (7·7m); (E, F) 26ft 8in (8·13m); length (A, G) 47ft 2in (14·38m); (B, D) 46ft 4in (14·12m); (E) 48ft 3¾in (14·73m); (F) 51ft 9¾in (15·80m); height (A, G) 13ft 2in (4·01m); (B, D) 13ft 1in (3·99m); (E, F) 13ft 4½in (4·08m).

Weights: Empty (A, G) 8,085lb (3667kg); (B, D) 8,361lb (3792kg); (E) 9,588lb (4349kg); (F) 9,700lb (4400kg); maximum loaded (A, G) 20,677lb (9379kg); (B, D) 20,500lb (9298kg); (E, F) 24,080lb (10,922kg).

Performance: Maximum speed at altitude (A, G) 925mph (1489km/h, Mach 1·40); (B, D) 885mph (1424km/h, Mach 1·34); (E) 1,060mph (1705km/h, Mach 1·60); initial climb (A, G) 28,700ft (8760m)/min; (B, D) 30,400ft (9265m)/min; (E) 31,600ft (9630m)/min; service ceiling (A, G) 50,500ft (15,390m); (B, D) 52,000ft (15,850m); (E) 54,000ft (16,460m); range with max fuel, with reserves, tanks retained, (A, G) 1,387 miles (2232km); (B, D) 1,393 miles (2241km); (E) 1,974 miles (3175km).

Armament: Two 20mm M-39A2 cannon each with 280 rounds in nose (can be retained in RF versions); five pylons for total external load of about 4,400lb (2000kg) in A, G (total military load for these models, including guns and ammunition, is 5,200lb) or 7,000lb (3175kg) in E; rails on wing-tips for AIM-9 Sidewinder missiles.

History: First flight (XT-38) 10 April 1959, (N-156F) 30 July 1959, (F-5A) 19 May 1964, (F-5E) 11 August 1972, (F-5F) 25 September 1974.

Users: (A, B, D, G) Brazil, Canada, Ethiopia, Greece, Iran, Jordan, S Korea, Libya, Malaysia, Morocco, Netherlands, Norway, Pakistan, Philippines, Saudi Arabia, Spain, Taiwan, Thailand, Turkey, USA (Air Force, not operational); (E, F) Brazil, Chile, Egypt, Ethiopia, Indonesia, Iran, Jordan, Kenya, Malaysia, Morocco, Peru, Philippines, Saudi Arabia, Singapore, S Korea, Sudan, Switzerland, Taiwan, Thailand, Tunisia, USA (Air Force, Navy), Vietnam (probably not operational).

Development: In 1955 Northrop began the project design of a lightweight fighter, known as Tally-Ho, powered by two J85 missile engines slung in pods under a very small unswept wing. It was yet another of the many projects born in the Korean era when pilots were calling for lighter, simpler fighters with higher performance. Gradually Welko Gasich and his team refined the design, putting the engines in the fuselage and increasing the size, partly to meet the needs of the Navy. In June 1956 the Navy had pulled out, while the Air Force ordered the trainer version as the T-38

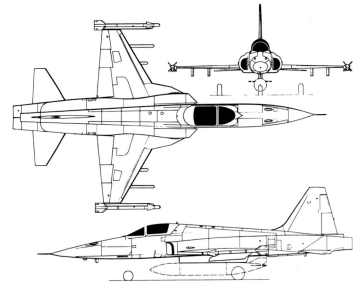

Three-view of F-5E Tiger II; the tandem-seat F-5F is 42in longer.

Talon. Over the next 15 years Northrop delivered 1,200 Talons, all to the USAF or. NASA, as the standard supersonic trainer of those services. With this assured programme the company took the unique decision to go ahead and build a demonstration fighter in the absence of any orders – the only time this has ever been done with a supersonic aircraft. By the time it was ready for flight in 1959 the N-156F, dubbed Freedom Fighter had received some US Defense funding, and the prototype carried US serial and stencil markings but no national markings. It was a simple little fighter, carrying about 485 gallons of fuel, two cannon and an old F-86 style sight, and having racks for two little Sidewinder missiles. Today such a prototype would have remained unsold, but in October 1962 the Department of Defense decided to buy the so-called Freedom Fighter in large numbers to give, or sell on advantageous terms, to anti-Communist nations. More than 1,040 of the Freedom Fighter (suffixes A, B, D, G) have been built, all but 178 being exports from Northrop. The Netherlands built the NF-5A and B equipment, heavier mission load, 500lb (227kg) more fuel in the longer fuselage, new inlet ducts, revised body and wing, root extensions and manoeuvring flaps and an X-band radar. Deliveries began in 1972, followed by the two-seat F in 1975. The US Air Force uses the Tiger II to equip its Tac Ftr Training Aggressor units, simulating hostile aircraft; the US Navy uses it as an Air Combat Trainer for future F-4 or F-14 pilots. Basic price of an E is considerably higher than that of the more powerful Jaguar (a recent sale was 12 for Kenya, priced at $70·6 million), but over 1,000 of the Tiger II type are likely to be supplied on attractive terms to many countries.

Left: An F-5A Freedom Fighter of the Hellenic (Greek) air force. These rather limited aircraft equip the 349ª Mira at Larissa and the 337ª, 341ª and 343ª all based at Nea Ankhialos near Volos. They have the advantage of good weather, vital for aircraft in this category.

Panavia Tornado

Tornado IDS (GR.1), ADV (F.2) and dual (T.3)

Origin: Panavia Aircraft GmbH, international company formed by British Aerospace, MBB of W Germany and Aeritalia.

Type: Two-seat multi-role combat aircraft, (S) optimised for strike, (AD) for air defence, (T) dual trainer.

Engines: Two Turbo-Union RB.199 Mk 101 three-shaft augmented turbofans each rated at 15,000lb (6800kg) with full afterburner.

Dimensions: Span (25°) 45ft 7¼in (13·90m), (65°) 28ft 2½in (8·60m); length (IDS) 54ft 9½in (16·7m), (ADV) 58ft 9in (17·9m); height 18ft 8½in (5·7m).

Weights: Empty, about 24,000lb (10,890kg); loaded (clean) about 35,000lb (15,880kg); maximum loaded, about 60,000lb (18,150kg).

Performance: Maximum speed (clean), at sea level, about 910mph (1465km/h, Mach 1·2), at height, over 1,320mph (2135km/h, Mach 2); service ceiling over 50,000ft (15,240m); range, about 1,000 miles (1610km) on internal fuel (high, wings spread), or over 3,000 miles (4830km) in ferry mode with maximum fuel.

Armament: Two 27mm Mauser cannon in lower forward fuselage; seven pylons, two tandem on body and four on the swinging wings, for external load up to 18,000lb (8165kg). ADV has only one MK27 gun, plus four Sky Flash missiles recessed under fuselage and two or four AIM-9L Sidewinder close-range missiles.

History: First flight (prototype) 14 August 1974), (production IDS) July 1979, (ADV) September 1979; service delivery (IDS to trials unit) February 1978, (squadron service, MFG) 1982.

Users: W Germany (Luftwaffe, Marineflieger), Italy, UK (RAF).

Development: No combat aircraft in history has ever been planned with such care by so many possible customers. Studies began in 1967, after the French had abandoned the AFVG aircraft in the same class and decided not to participate in collaborative aircraft of this type. Panavia Aircraft was registered on 26 March 1969 in Munich as a three-nation company to manage the MRCA (multi-role combat aircraft) programme, with shares

Above: Two MBB-assembled prototypes: white-painted 04 and camouflaged 07, later joined by other pre-production machines and production IDS.

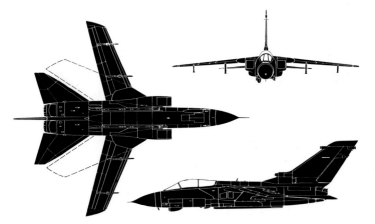

Three-view of Tornado IDS (interdictor/strike) variant.

held in the ratio BAC 42½ per cent, MBB 42½ per cent and Aeritalia 15 per cent. In September 1969, after intense competition with the United States, the RB.199 was selected as the engine and a month later Turbo-Union was formed as the engine-management company with shares held in the ratio Rolls-Royce 40 per cent. MTU 40 per cent and Fiat 20 per cent. Thanks to careful planning the Tornado programme has since demonstrated that it is possible for several nations to work together to create a modern military aircraft which promises to exceed all possible rivals in mission effectiveness, versatility and low cost, having already demonstrated better mission capability than the latest competing types designed specifically for that mission. Its design missions are: close air support/battlefield interdiction; long-range interdiction/strike; naval strike; air superiority; air defence/interception; reconnaissance; training. At one time it was planned that the three nations should develop slightly different versions with either one or two seats and dry or wet wings, but all basic aircraft now in production are identical, with two seats and sealed integral-tank wings. From stem to stern the Tornado is totally modern — a fact which its many competitors have sought to counter by claiming it to be "complicated" or "expensive". In fact it is not possible to fly the required missions without carrying the equipment, and the fly-away price of £3·9 million (in September 1974 sterling) is by a very wide margin cheaper than any comparable aircraft. The only aircraft that bears comparison with MRCA is the larger F-14, which cannot meet the MRCA requirements in the attack and reconnaissance roles, and is officially doubted as having the capability — in the European environment — to fly the interception missions of the Tornado ADV. Other combat aircraft with a single seat and non-swinging wing are grossly deficient in all ▶

Below: Prototype 02, assembled in Britain in 1974, with 'tri-national' markings, original tail/body fairing and camera on the front of the passive-ECM fairing.

Nosing in over its home airfield – Warton, on the north shore of the Ribble estuary – the first Tornado F.2 interceptor gives a hint of its outstanding capabilities. Two engines (of amazing compactness and fuel-economy), two crew, a new advanced-technology radar, swing wings, extra fuel (in a longer fuselage), the world's most modern sensors and cockpit displays, and Skyflash and (not fitted here) AIM-9L missiles form an unequalled combination.

roles except close-range air combat, a specialised mission for which the common version of Tornado is not intended (though its performance in this role is considerably better than a Mirage III, F-5 or F-4).

The basic Tornado has highly compact and efficient engines of extremely advanced design, with automatically scheduled inlets and nozzles. Flight control is by large tailerons, augmented at low sweep angles by wing spoilers; the system is fully digital and signalled by quad fly-by-wire via an automatic command and stability augmentation system. For high lift at low speeds the wings have full-span slats and double-slotted flaps. Other equipment includes a mapping radar, terrain-following radar and computer, and laser target ranger for extreme accuracy. ECM and other penetration aids are exceptional. Planned production for the three original partners comprises 809 aircraft, of which 385 will be for the RAF, 202 for the Luftwaffe (replacing the F-104G and G91R), 122 for the Marineflieger (replacing the F-104G) and 100 for the Regia Aeronautica (replacing the F-104G and G91Y) in all roles. The variety of external stores to be carried by MRCA exceeds that for any other aircraft in history, embracing almost every airborne store of three major nations in virtually all combat roles. A proportion of aircraft for the first three customers will be dual trainers (the first flew on 5 August 1975) which retain all the fuel capacity and weapons of single-pilot versions.

Of the RAF total of 385, about 220 will be of the common IDS (inter-

Above: Initial gun-firing trials took place in April 1978 with prototype 06 (the gun had been air-tested in a Lightning).

Left: Another photograph of 06, which was the first to fly stores-separation tests, a task completed in March 1976.

Below: First launch from Tornado of a Kormoran anti-ship guided missile took place from 09 at Decimomannu in July 1978.

diction strike) variant; the other 165 will be of the ADV (air-defence variant) type, planned to replace the Phantom in the air defence of the UK. Commonality with the IDS aircraft is officially put at 80 per cent, differences mainly being confined to the forward fuselage though the wing-root gloves have acute sweep and no Krüger flaps. Engines are unchanged, though higher-thrust versions are available on customer request. The ADV fuselage is longer partly to accommodate Sparrow or Sky Flash missiles nose-to-tail and partly to accommodate much additional fuel. The radar is a completely new Marconi Foxhunter set, with planar scanner by Ferranti inside a more pointed radome which reduces drag. Computer and radar programs are quite different from those of the IDS, though each version has considerable capability in the primary role of the other. Great attention has been paid to the ADV target identification and vision-augmenting subsystems, to make full use of the range of the radar and Sky Flash missile. The radar homing/warning installation is also new, and quite different from equipment fits used on the IDS version.

In mid-1979 the 16 prototype and pre-production Tornados had flown and been succeeded by the first few production machines (the first two being dual-pilot versions with full operational capability) and the first ADV prototypes. At that time three contracts for production batches had been signed for a total of 314 aircraft for inventory service with the four initial customers.

Rockwell International OV-10 Bronco

OV-10A to -10E

Origin: Rockwell International Corp, USA.

Type: (Except B) two-seat multi-role counter-insurgency; (B) target tug.

Engines: (Except B(Z)) two 715ehp AiResearch T76-410/411 single-shaft centrifugal turboprops; (B(Z)) as other versions plus General Electric J85-4 turbojet of 2,950lb (1338kg) thrust above fuselage.

Dimensions: Span 40ft (12·19m); length (except D) 41ft 7in (12·67m); (D) 44ft (13·4m); height 15ft 2in (4·62m).

Weights: Empty (A) 6,969lb (3161kg); maximum loaded (A) 14,466lb (6563kg).

Performance: Maximum speed (A, sea level, clean) 281mph (452km/h); initial climb 2,300ft (700m)/min; (B(Z)) 6,800ft/min; service ceiling 30,000ft (9150m); range with maximum weapon load, about 600 miles (960km); ferry range at 12,000lb gross, 1,428 miles (2300km).

Armament: Four 7·62mm M60C machine guns in sponsons; 1,200lb (544kg) hardpoint on centreline and four 600lb (272kg) points under sponsons; one Sidewinder missile rail under each wing; (OV-10D) as other versions plus three-barrel 20mm cannon in remotely aimed ventral power turret.

History: First flight 16 July 1965; (production OV-10A) 6 August 1967; (YOV-10D) 9 June 1970.

Users: W Germany, Indonesia, S Korea, Thailand, USA (Air Force, Marine Corps), Venezuela.

Development: Recognising that no US aircraft was tailored to the urgent task of fighting Co-In (counter-insurgency) operations, or "brush-fire wars", the US Department of Defense in 1960 began study of the problem and in 1962 issued a joint USAF/Navy/Marine Corps specification for a Light Armed Reconnaissance Aircraft (LARA). The winner, in 1964, was

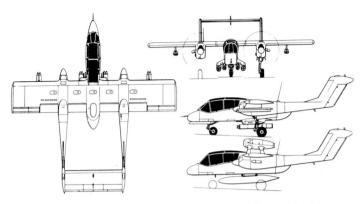

Above: Three-view of OV-10A with side view (bottom) of OV-10B(Z).

the Bronco. Designed to operate from short rough strips (or on floats or skis) it can carry a wide range of tactical equipment and weapons, including doppler radar, TV reconnaissance, five paratroops or two casualties. The OV-10A was ordered in October 1966 and by 1969 the Marine Corps had 114, while the USAF were using 157 for Forward Air Control (FAC) duties in Vietnam. In 1969 Pave Nail Conversion of 15 aircraft fitted them with laser rangers, stabilized night sighting system, Loran and other devices for night FAC, attack or target illumination for other aircraft. The B and jet-boosted B(Z) are used by the Luftwaffe. The OV-10D has Night Observation Gunship (NOGS) equipment, with long-nosed IR sensor, cannon turret and, as a conversion, 1,000ehp T76 engines.

Below: Almost identical to the basic American OV-10A is the OV-10F, 16 of which were supplied to Indonesia. They equip one squadron dedicated to counter-insurgent duties, though the aircraft is also equipped for the carriage of 3,200lb (1452kg) of cargo, five parachute troops or two stretcher casualties.

Saab 35 Draken

J35A, B, D and F, Sk35C, S35E and export versions

Origin: Saab-Scania AB, Linköping, Sweden.

Type: (J35) single-seat all-weather fighter-bomber; (Sk35) dual trainer; (S35) single-seat all-weather reconnaissance.

Engine: One Svenska Flygmotor RM6 (licence-built Rolls-Royce Avon with SFA afterburner): (A, B, C) 15,000lb (6804kg) RM6B; (D, E, F and export) 17,110lb (7761kg) RM6C.

Dimensions: Span 30ft 10in (9·4m); length 50ft 4in (15·4m) (S35E, 52ft); height 12ft 9in (3·9m).

Weights: Empty (D) 16,017lb; (F) 18,180lb (8250kg); maximum loaded (A) 18,200lb; (D) 22,663lb; (F) 27,050lb (12,270kg); (F-35) 35,275lb (16,000kg).

Performance: Maximum speed (D onwards, clean) 1,320mph (2125km/h, Mach 2·0), (with two drop tanks and two 1,000lb bombs) 924mph (1487 km/h, Mach 1·4); initial climb (D onwards, clean) 34,450ft (10,500m)/min; service ceiling (D onwards, clean) about 65,000ft (20,000m); range (internal fuel plus external weapons, typical) 800 miles (1300km), (maximum fuel) 2,020 miles (3250km).

Armament: (A) two 30mm Aden M/55 in wings, four Rb 324 (Side-winder) missiles; (B) as A plus attack ordnance to maximum of 2,200lb (1000kg); (C) none; (D) as B; (E) usually none but provision as A; (F) one 30mm Aden plus two Rb27 Falcon (radar) and two Rb28 Falcon (infra-red) missiles, plus two or four Rb324; (F-35) two 30mm Aden plus nine stores pylons each rated at 1,000lb (454kg) all usable simultaneously, plus four Rb324.

History: First flight 25 October 1955; (production J35A) 15 February 1958; final delivery (35XS) 1975, (Danish TF-35) 1976.

Users: Denmark, Finland, Sweden (RSAF).

Development: Again in advance of any other country in Western Europe, the Saab 35 was designed in 1949–51 as an all-weather supersonic fighter able to use small airfields. Erik Bratt and his team arrived at the unique "double delta" shape after studying different ways of packaging the fuel and equipment, the best arrangement being with items one behind the other

Right: One of the last of more than 600 Drakens was this TF-35XD, one of six of this versatile two-seat dual-control version to be supplied to the Danish air force in 1968–73 along with 20 of the formidable 35XD single-seat version.

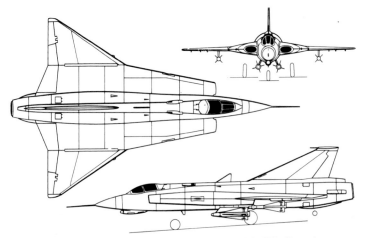

Above: Three-view of the Falcon-armed J35F ("Filip" to the Swedish Air Force).

giving a long aircraft of very small frontal area. In 1960 attack wing F13 found the A (Adam) simple to fly and maintain, sensitive in pitch and yet virtually unbreakable. B (Bertil) was more complex, with S7 collision-course fire control integrated with the Swedish Stril 60 air defence environment. Most Sk35C trainers were converted Adams. D (David) was first to reach Mach 2, despite continual increases in weight mainly due to fuel capacity raised from 493 to 680 gallons. E (Erik) carries French OMERA cameras and in 1973 was updated with external British Vinten night/low-level pods. F (Filip) is an automatic interceptor with Ericsson (Hughes basis) radar of pulse-doppler type. Production was closed at 606 with 40 multi-role F-35/RF-35/TF-35 aircraft for Denmark and 12 XS for Finland assembled by Valmet Oy.

Left: The first version to enter service was the J35A, popularly called 'Adam' in the Swedish air force. This example, one of the first to be delivered to F13 (the Bravalla Flygflottilj) at Nörrkoping in March 1960, is seen with Rb 324 Sidewinders in place.

Saab 37 Viggen

AJ37, JA37, SF37, SH37 and Sk37

Origin: Saab-Scania AB, Linköping, Sweden.

Type: (AJ) single-seat all-weather attack; (JA) all-weather fighter; (SF) armed photo-reconnaissance; (SH) armed sea surveillance; (SK) dual trainer.

Engine: One Svenska Flygmotor RM8 (licence-built Pratt & Whitney JT8D two-shaft turbofan redesigned in Sweden for Mach 2 and fitted with SFA afterburner); (AJ, SF, SH and Sk) 25,970lb (11,790kg) RM8A; (JA) 28,086lb (12,750kg) RM8B.

Dimensions: Span of main wing 34ft 9¼in (10·6m); length (AJ) 53ft 5¾in (16·3m); (JA37 with probe) 53ft 11in; height 18ft 4½in (5·6m).

Weights: Not disclosed, except AJ37 "normal armament" gross weight of 35,275lb (16,000kg).

Performance: Maximum speed (clean) about 1,320mph (2135km/h, Mach 2), or Mach 1·1 at sea level; initial climb, about 40,000ft (12,200m)/min (time from start of take-off run to 32,800ft—10,000m = 100sec); service ceiling, over 60,000ft (18,300m); tactical radius with external stores (not drop tanks), hi-lo-hi profile, over 620 miles (1000km).

Armament: Seven pylons (option: nine) for aggregate external load of 13,200lb (6000kg), including Rb04E or Rb05A missiles for attack, and Rb27, Rb28 and Rb324 missiles for defence. In addition the JA37 has a 30mm Oerlikon KCA gun and will carry "new long- and short-range missiles for air-to-air interception"; Skyflash is being evaluated.

History: First flight 8 February 1967; (production AJ) 23 February 1971; service delivery (AJ) June 1971.

User: Sweden (RSAF).

Development: Yet again blazing a trail ahead of other nations, the Royal Swedish Air Board planned System 37 in 1958–61 as a standardized weapon system to be integrated with the Stril 60 air-defence environment of radars, computers and displays. Included in the system is a standard platform (in this case a supersonic manned aircraft) produced in five

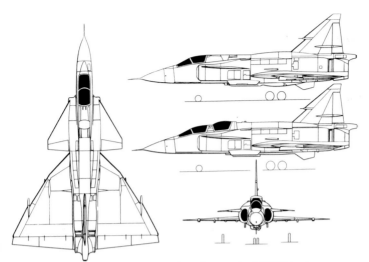

Three-view of JA37, with side view (centre) of SK37 trainer.

versions each tailored to a specific task. Thanks to a unique configuration with a 400 sq ft wing preceded by a canard foreplane with trailing-edge flaps, the Viggen (Thunderbolt) has outstanding STOL (short take-off and landing) performance and excellent turn radius at all speeds. Efficient and prolonged operations are possible from narrow strips 500m (1,640ft) in length, such as stretches of highway. Equipment in all versions includes headup display, autothrottle/speed control on approach, no-flare landing autopilot and thrust reverser. The AJ operates camouflaged in attack wings F7, F15 and F6, with production continuing in 1977 on a mix of AJ, SF, SH ►

Now in service with the Flygvapen F13 wing at Norrköping, the JA37 is an outstanding all-weather fighter, seen here with belly gun pod, instrumentation pod, two BAe Dynamics Sky Flash missiles and three Swedish-made RB24 Sidewinder missiles.

and Sk models. At the beginning of the year about 145 had been delivered of the total orders for 180 of these versions. During 1976 Viggens in RSAF service were grounded until the cause of inflight structural (wing) failures had been fully explained and aircraft rectified. Apart from this the Viggen has proved as outstanding as it looked on paper in the 1960s, and even today no other Western European aircraft can rival it for radar performance, flight performance and short field length in all weathers. The latest Viggen variant, the JA37, is considerably different, with a new engine, very powerful gun, UAP 1023 pulse-doppler radar, digital automatic flight control system and extremely advanced inertial measurement and central computer systems. The development effort for the JA37 rivals that for the complete original aircraft, but with the help of a fleet of special-purpose test aircraft (some new and most rebuilds of early AJ and other models) the JA was cleared for production in 1976. By the start of 1977 most of the initial batch of 30 were on the line, and service delivery is due in 1978. Eventually 200 are to equip eight squadrons.

**Above: Afterburning takeoff of one of the
original AJ37 attack aircraft.**

**Left: A display of weapons in front of an AJ37,
with RB04E missiles on the aircraft.**

**Below: The SK37 is the tandem-seat dual-
control trainer, able to carry AJ37 weapons.**

SEPECAT Jaguar

Jaguar GR.1 and T.2, Jaguar A and E, and Jaguar International

Origin: SEPECAT, consortium formed by British Aerospace (BAC) and Dassault-Breguet, France.

Type: (GR.1, A and International (I.)) single-seat all-weather attack; (T.2 and E) dual operational trainer.

Engines: Two Rolls-Royce/Turboméca Adour two-shaft augmented turbofans: (except I.) 7,305lb (3313kg) Adour 102; (I.) 8,000lb (3630kg) Adour 804.

Dimensions: Span 28ft 6in (8·69m); length (except T.2, E) 50ft 11in (15·52m); (T.2, E) 53ft 11in (16·42m); height 16ft 1½in (4·92m).

Weights: Empty, classified but about 15,000lb (6800kg); "normal take-off" (ie, internal fuel and some external ordnance) 23,000lb (10,430kg); maximum loaded 34,000lb (15,500kg).

Performance: Maximum speed (lo, some external stores) 820mph (1320km/h, Mach 1·1), (hi, some external stores) 1,055mph (1700km/h, Mach 1·6); climb and ceiling, classified; attack radius, no external fuel, hi-lo-hi with bombs, 507 miles (815km); ferry range 2,614 miles (4210km).

Armament: (A, E) two 30mm DEFA 553 each with 150 rounds; five pylons for total external load of 10,000lb (4536kg); (GR.1) as above but guns two 30mm Aden; (T.2) as above but single Aden. (International) wide range of options including increased external loads.

History: First flight (E) 8 September 1968; (production E) 2 November 1971; (production GR.1) 11 October 1972; squadron delivery (E, A) May 1972, (GR, T) June 1973.

Users: Ecuador, France, India, Oman, UK (RAF).

Development: Developed jointly by BAC in Britain and Dassault-Breguet in France, to meet a joint requirement of the Armée de l'Air and RAF, the

Right: RAF Jaguar GR.1 of 54 Sqn, based at Coltishall.

Below: A Jaguar GR.1 of RAF 20 Sqn pictured at dusk near its shelter at Brüggen.

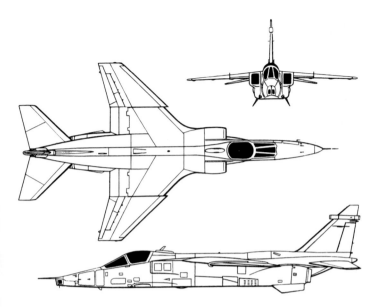

Above: Three-view of Jaguar GR.1 without stores.

Jaguar is a far more powerful and effective aircraft than originally planned and has already demonstrated unmatched capabilities in service. The original idea was a light trainer and close-support machine, with 1,300lb

continued ▶

Left: One of the basically simple Jaguar A attack aircraft of the French Armée de l'Air.

XZ358 was one of the last of the 202 Jaguars delivered to the Royal Air Force. It is a GR.1 multi-role single-seater, pictured here making an afterburning takeoff in clean condition. By late 1980 almost all the aircraft in service will be fitted with more powerful Mk 104 engines of the same thrust as the Mk 804 fitted to the Jaguar International export version.

weapon load, but with British pressure this was upgraded to today's outstanding aircraft whose only marketing problem is the fact that the French partner prefers aircraft which appear to be all-French (yet, in fact, Dassault makes only the same proportion of the Mirage F1 as it does of the Jaguar, namely, about 50 per cent). Despite this unhappy political scene the sheer merit of the Jaguar, and the enthusiastic missionary work done by its operating units in the Armée de l'Air and RAF, is gradually winning valuable orders, beginning with Ecuador and Oman in 1974. Further sales are likely with the more powerful International version now flying. The two basic single-seat versions share a common airframe but are totally different in equipment. The French A model has a simple twin-gyro platform, doppler, and a basic navigation computer; in 1977 an Atlis laser pod was being added. The RAF GR.1 has inertial navigation, head-up display, projected map display, radar height, integrated nav/attack system and laser ranger, as well as comprehensive ECM and option of a multi-sensor reconnaissance pod. All versions can have nose radar, refuelling probe and the option of overwing pylons for light dogfight missiles (Jaguar development aircraft have flown with Matra Magics in these positions). Thanks to a dynamic programme of engine development Jaguar users have the option of various increased-thrust Adours, including the Mk 804 (Adour 26) fitted to the basic Jaguar International, and the even more powerful Adour 56 and 58 (in the 10,000lb, 4500kg class) which will be available from 1980. It is the intention of the RAF to select one of the uprated engines and convert all Jaguar engines to this standard, to gain even better field length and flight performance with large mission loads. By 1977 some 300 aircraft had been delivered, and several new customers were engaged in contract negotiation.

Right: This Jaguar International is one of ten single-seaters (as illustrated) and two two-seaters equipping No 8 Sqn of the Sultan of Oman's Air Force. This unit is normally based at Thumrayt, in Dhofar province, and is dedicated to long-range ground attack with various weapons and to air combat with Magic missiles on overwing pylons.

Below: Test firing of a Matra 550 Magic close-range air-to-air missile from special overwing pylons added to a Jaguar retained for research and trials programmes by British Aerospace Warton Division. Another completed programme concerns fitting the Thomson-CSF Agave radar, and many other sensors are available as options.

Above: Fly-past by single-seat Jaguar A and two-seat Jaguar E aircraft of the 7e Escadre de Chasse, Armée de l'Air, normally based at St Dizier. This was the first Jaguar wing to be fully equipped in the French air force, with a strength of 35 single-seaters and 25 dual-control trainers with the conversion unit.

Shenyang F-6 bis

F-6bis (NATO code name "Fantan A")

Origin: State Aircraft Factory, Shenyang, People's Republic of China.
Type: All-weather fighter, attack and reconnaissance aircraft.
Engines: Two axial turbojets with afterburners (see text).
Dimensions (estimated): Span 33ft 5in (10·2m); length 50ft (15·25m); height 11ft (3·35m).
Weights: (estimated) Empty 13,670lb (6200kg); loaded (clean) 20,285lb (9200kg), (maximum) 23,600lb (10,700kg).
Performance (estimated): Maximum speed, clean (sea level) about 760mph (1225km/h, Mach 1), (high altitude) about 1,190mph (1910km/h, Mach 1·8); combat radius (hi-lo-hi, two bombs, two tanks) 500 miles (800km).
Armament: Not known, but almost certainly includes internal guns, external stores pylons for tanks and ordnance and comprehensive ECM equipment.
History: First flight, possibly 1968; service delivery, probably early 1970s.
Users: People's Republic of China (AF, Navy), Egypt (?).

Development: Obviously derived from the F-6, the Chinese-built MiG-19SF, the F-6bis represents the first (enforced) attempt by the Shenyang-based home industry to produce combat aircraft independently. Despite extreme difficulties caused by a lack of industrial backing and skilled labour, the production of nationally developed aircraft was forced on the PRC (People's Republic of China) by its isolation from technically advanced nations and imminence of the Soviet threat. The excellent qualities of the MiG-19 basic design eventually led to the F-6 being chosen for development in preference to the F-7, the illegally manufactured MiG-21PF. During the 1960s the Shenyang F-6bis took shape as an enlarged F-6 with lateral inlet ducts feeding direct to the two engines (a Chinese illustration suggests that the mid-wing has been retained, with ducts above and below), leaving the nose free for a large search radar of unknown type. The sketch referred to showed no wing cannon, but the two 30mm NR-30s of the F-6 have probably been retained in view of the great length of inlet duct ahead of the wing, interfering with pilot view. The inlets are apparently simple and non-variable, efficient at low level but limiting high-altitude Mach number. The radar could be a derivative of the "Spin Scan B" as used in later North Vietnamese MiG-21PF fighters sent via China, but in the author's opinion

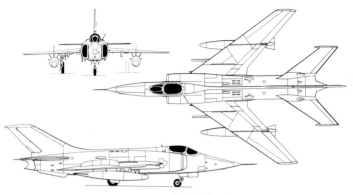

Above: Three-view of Shenyang F-6bis Fantan.

is more likely to be a copy of the much more powerful AWG-10 or APQ-109 fitted to Phantoms of the late 1960s. Whether the PRC has also copied Sparrow and/or Sidewinder is problematical.

In his Fiscal Year 1977 report the US SecDef (then Donald Rumsfeld) described the "Fantan-A" as a principal tactical aircraft of the PRC Navy; earlier it was known to be in service with the PRCAF. Compared with the F-6 it should be a considerably more effective machine, provided engine power has risen at least in proportion to the weight. Some Western reports suggest that the engines are the Tumansky RD-9B-811, of 8,270lb (3750kg) maximum thrust; in the author's view an equally plausible possibility is that the bigger and more powerful R-11 engine of the F-7 (13,120lb, 5950kg) could have been chosen. Indeed use of this engine in the F-9 might in some degree explain the early termination of Chinese production of the F-7. As this book went to press little is known of the F-6bis and it could even be subject to severe problems and limitations. It should in any case not be confused with the entirely different combat aircraft (believed to be a twin-engined delta) which will be powered by the Chinese-assembled Rolls-Royce Spey.

Below left: A line-up of F-6bis attack aircraft of the Air Force of the People's Liberation Army of China.

Below: Bombs falling from the wing pylons of an F-6bis which also appears to have open weapon-bay doors (also seen at left).

Soko Galeb and Jastreb

G2-A, Galeb, J-1 Jastreb

Origin: "Soko" Metalopreradivacka Industrija, Yugoslavia.
Type: (Galeb) dual armed trainer; Jastreb, single-seat attack.
Engine: One Rolls-Royce Viper single-shaft turbojet; (G) 2,500lb (1134kg) thrust Mk 22-6; (J) 3,000lb (1360kg) Mk 531.
Dimensions: Span (excluding tip tanks) 34ft 4½in (10·47m); (J) 34ft 8in; length 33ft 11in (10·34m); (J) 35ft 1½in; height 10ft 9in (3·28m); (J) 11ft 11½in.
Weights: Empty 5,775lb (2620kg); (J) 6,217lb maximum loaded 9,210lb (4178kg); (G, clean, fully aerobatic) 7,438lb; (J) 10,287lb.
Performance: Maximum speed 505mph (812km/h); (J) 510mph; initial climb 4,500ft (1370m)/min; service ceiling 39,375ft (12,000m); range (hi, max fuel) 770 miles (1240km); (J) 945 miles.
Armament: (G) 12·7mm guns in nose, each with 80 rounds; underwing pylons for two 220lb (100kg) bombs, or light loads of rockets. (J) three 12·7mm in nose, each with 135 rounds; eight underwing hardpoints, two furthest inboard carrying stores of 551lb (250kg), the rest single 127mm rockets.
History: First flight (G) May 1961; service delivery (G) 1965.
Users: Libya, Yugoslavia, Zambia.

Development: The first Yugoslav jet to go into production, the tandem-

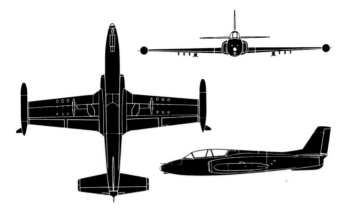

Above: Three-view of Soko G2-A Galeb (TJ-1 similar).

seat Galeb (Seagull) has been fully developed and built in modest numbers for the Yugoslav Air Force and Zambia. Pupil and instructor sit in Folland lightweight seats, and an air-conditioning system is an option. The Jastreb (Hawk) uses a similar airframe, with local strengthening for the more powerful engine and heavier external stores. Again Zambia has received an export version, but without the optional cabin pressurization and self-contained engine-start system. Jastrebs can carry cameras in the fuselage and in the nose of the tip tanks, and also tow an aerial target.

Left: This echelon of Jastrebs shows the basic J-1 attack version in service with the Yugoslav Air Force. This model has nose armament of three 'fifty-calibre' Colt-Browning guns and a total of eight underwing pylons for various stores. There are also RJ-1 reconnaissance and various export versions. All have the Viper 531 engine, as does the tandem-seat Jastreb trainer which looks very similar to the lower-powered Galeb.

Below: First flown in 1961, the Soko G2-A Galeb has been made in appreciable numbers both for the Yugoslav Air Force and for export. Normal armament comprises two heavy machine guns of familiar Colt-Browning type, plus light bomb, rocket and other loads under the wings. Now supplementing this type in service, the TJ-1 (trainer Jastreb) has the single-seat Jastreb's more powerful self-starting engine and additional avionics.

Sukhoi Su-7

Su-7B, -7BM, -7BMK and -7U; NATO name "Fitter"

Origin: The design bureau of Pavel A. Sukhoi, Soviet Union.

Type: Single-seat close-support and interdiction; (-7U) dual-control trainer.

Engine: One Lyulka AL-7F turbojet rated at 15,430lb (7000kg) dry or 22,046lb (10,000kg) with maximum afterburner.

Dimensions: Span 29ft 3½in (8·93m), length (all, incl probe) 57ft (17·37m); height (all) 15ft 5in (4·70m).

Weights: Empty (typical -7) 19,000lb (8620kg), maximum loaded (typical -7) 30,000lb (13,610kg).

Performance: Maximum speed, clean, at altitude, (all) 1,055mph (1700km/h, Mach 1·6), initial climb (-7BM) 29,000ft (9120m)/min; service ceiling (-7BM) 49,700ft (15,150m); range with twin drop tanks (all) 900 miles (1450km).

Armament: (-7) two 30mm NR-30 cannon, each with 70 rounds, in wing roots; four wing pylons, inners rated at 1,653lb (750kg) and outers at 1,102lb (500kg), but when two tanks are carried on fuselage pylons total external weapon load is reduced to 2,205lb (1000kg).

History: First flight (-7 prototype) not later than 1955; service delivery (-7B) 1959.

Users: (-7) Afghanistan, Algeria, Czechoslovakia, Egypt, Hungary, India, Iraq, N Korea, Poland, Romania, Soviet Union, Syria, Vietnam.

Development: Two of the wealth of previously unknown Soviet aircraft revealed at the 1956 Aviation Day at Tushino were large Sukhoi fighters, one with a swept wing (called "Fitter" by NATO) and the other a tailed delta (called "Fishpot"). Both were refined into operational types, losing some of their commonality in the process. The delta entered service as the Su-9 and -11, described separately. The highly-swept Su-7 was likewise built in very large numbers, optimised not for air superiority but for ground

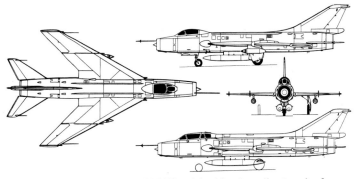

Above: Three-view of Su-7BMK, with side view (bottom) of -7U "Moujik".

attack. As such it has found a worldwide market, and despite severe short-comings has been exported in numbers which exceed 700. All Sukhoi combat aircraft have been made within the Soviet Union. The good points of the Su-7 family are robust structure, reasonable reliability and low cost; drawbacks are vulnerability to small-calibre fire and the impossibility of getting adequate field length, weapon load and radius of action all together. There are many variants. The original -7B was quickly superseded by the more powerful -7BM, with twin ribbon tail chutes. The most common export model is the -7BMK with low-pressure tyres and other changes to improve behaviour from short unpaved strips. The -7U is the tandem dual trainer. Since 1964 many BMK have been seen with take-off rockets and four wing pylons.

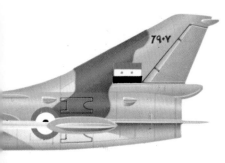

Left: An Su-7BM of the Egyptian Air Force. Some 120 survive, despite heavy losses from many causes.

Below: A frame from a Soviet propaganda film showing Su-7B type attack aircraft making passes on surface targets. The fundamental fault of this family is ability to carry fuel or weapons but not both.

Sukhoi Su-9 and Su-11

Su-9 "Fishpot B", Su-9U "Maiden" and Su-11 "Fishpot C".

Origin: The design bureau named for Pavel O. Sukhoi, Soviet Union.

Type: Single-seat all-weather interceptor (Su-9U, two-seat trainer).

Engine: One Lyulka single-shaft turbojet with afterburner; (Su-9 and -9U) AL-7F rated at 19,840lb (9000kg) thrust with maximum afterburner, (Su-11) AL-7F-1 rated at 22,046lb (10,000kg).

Dimensions: Span 27ft 8in (8·43m); length (-9, -9U) about 54ft (16·5m), (-11) 57ft (17·4m); height 16ft (4·9m).

Weights: (All, estimated) empty 20,000lb (9070kg); loaded (typical mission) 27,000lb (12,250kg), (maximum) 30,000lb (13,610kg).

Performance: (-11, estimated) maximum speed (clean, sea level) 720mph (1160km/h, Mach 0·95), (clean, optimum height) 1,190mph (1910km/h, Mach 1·8), (two missiles and two tanks at optimum height) 790mph (1270km/h, Mach 1·2); initial climb 27,000ft (8230m)/min; service ceiling (clean) 55,700ft (17,000m); range (two missiles, two tanks) about 700 miles (1125km).

Armament: (-9) four AA-1 "Alkali" air-to-air missiles; (-9U) same as -9, or not fitted; (-11) two AA-3 "Anab" air-to-air missiles, one radar and the other IR.

History: First flight (-9) before 1956; (-11) probably 1966; service delivery (-9) probably 1959, (-11) 1967.

User: Soviet Union (IA-PVO).

Development: When first seen, at the 1956 Tushino display, one prototype delta-winged Sukhoi fighter had a small conical radome above the plain

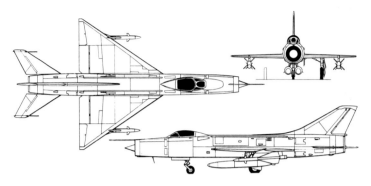

Above: Three-view of Su-11, with "Anab" missiles.

nose inlet, while a second had a conical centrebody. The latter arrangement was chosen for production as the Su-9, though development was rather protracted. At first sharing the same engine installation, rear fuselage and tail as the original Su-7, the Su-9 eventually came to have no parts exactly common. No gun was ever seen on an Su-9 by Western intelligence, the primitive missiles being the only armament. At least 2,000 were built, an additional number, probably supplemented by conversions, being tandem-seat dual trainers with a cockpit slightly different from that of the Su-7U. The Su-11 is cleaned up in every part of the airframe, has a longer and less-tapered nose with larger radar centrebody, completely different armament (still without guns) and a fuselage similar to the Su-7B with external duct fairings along the top on each side. Though much larger and more powerful than the MiG-21, these interceptors have an almost identical tailed-delta configuration. Unlike the MiG-21 they have all-weather capability (interpreted as "night and rain" rather than true all-weather), but are still limited in radius, endurance and armament. In 1976 they were together judged to equip one-quarter of the 2,500-strong interceptor force of the IA-PVO, but were being replaced by the Su-15 and MiG-23S.

Left: A frame from a film showing both inner 'Alkali' missiles being fired from an Su-9 of the PVO.

Below: Large numbers of Su-11 interceptors still operate with the IA-PVO, though probably no longer in the most sensitive spots.

Sukhoi Su-15

Versions known to the West are code-named "Flagon-A to -E"

Origin: The design bureau of Pavel O. Sukhoi, Soviet Union.

Type: Most versions, all-weather interceptor.

Engines: Two afterburning engines, believed to be Tumansky R-13F2 turbojets each rated at about 12,000lb (5443kg) dry and 15,875lb (7200kg) with afterburner.

Dimensions: Span (A) 31ft 3in (9·50m), (D) about 36ft (11·0m); length (all) 70ft 6in (21·50m); height 16ft 6in (5·0m).

Weights: (Estimated) empty (A) 24,000lb (10,900kg), (D) 26,000lb (11,800kg); normal loaded (A) 35,275lb (16,000kg); maximum loaded (D) 46,000lb (21,000kg).

Performance: (Estimated) maximum speed at altitude, with two missiles, 1,520mph (2445km/h, Mach 2·3); initial climb 35,000ft (10,670m)/min; service ceiling 65,000ft (19,800m); combat radius 450 miles (725km); ferry range about 1,400 miles (2250km).

Armament: Two underwing pylons normally carry one radar "Anab" and one infra-red "Anab"; two fuselage pylons normally carry drop tanks, often with a 23mm GSh-23 two-barrel cannon between them; other missiles such as AA-6 or AA-7 are probably now being carried (but not yet seen by the West).

History: First flight (Su-15 prototype) probably 1964; (production Su-15) probably 1967.

User: Soviet Union (PVO).

Development: Following naturally on from the Su-11, and strongly resembling earlier aircraft in wings and tail, the Su-15 has two engines which not only confer increased performance but also leave the nose free for a large AI radar. The initial "Flagon-A" version entered IA-PVO Strany service in 1969. "Flagon-B" is a STOL rough-field version with three lift jets in the fuselage and a revised "double delta" wing. "Flagon-C" is the Su-15U dual trainer. "-D" is basically a "-B" without lift jets, and "-E" has completely updated electronics and the same extended wing but with further leading-edge improvements; the latest and probably final version is "Flagon-F" with an ogival radome suggesting use of a larger

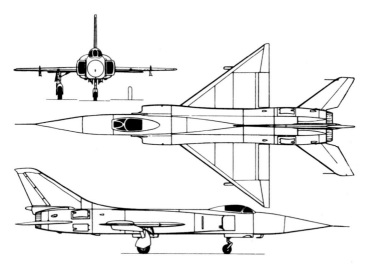

Above: Three-view of "Flagon A" Su-15 without missiles.

aerial and possibly a completely new radar. It has been speculated that some late examples have an internal gun. In 1971 a US official estimated that 400 Su-15 were in service, with production at about 15 monthly. In early 1976 an estimate of PVO establishment gave the number of all Su-15 versions in combat service as 600. Though small numbers have served in Warsaw Pact countries and, in 1973, in Egypt, all Su-15s are at present believed to serve with the IA-PVO. There has been speculation in the West that later models could carry the Fox Fire radar and AA-6 "Acrid" missiles of the MiG-25.

Above: This experimental STOL aircraft appeared publicly in 1967. It introduced a compound-taper wing very similar to that on all versions now in service ('Flagon-E' and '-F') as well as three lift jets in a special bay in the centre fuselage (note open lift-bay doors above fuselage). Normal Su-15s need a paved runway.

Left: IA-PVO officers clustered round the cockpit of one of the current operational versions, either a 'Flagon-E' or a 'Flagon-F', the latter having a modified radome. Rather un-Russian in having immense power but very little wing (relative to gross weight), about 1,000 of all versions are in use.

Sukhoi Su-17 and Su-20

Su-17 "Fitter C", Su-20 and Su-22

Origin: The design bureau named for Pavel O. Sukhoi, Soviet Union.
Type: Single-seat attack and close-support aircraft.
Engine: (-17) one Lyulka AL-21F-3 single-shaft turbojet with afterburner rated at 17,200lb (7800kg) dry and 25,000lb (11,340kg) with maximum afterburner, (-20, -22) believed to be AL-7F-1 rated at 22,046lb (10,000kg).
Dimensions (all): Span (28°) 45ft 11$\frac{1}{4}$in (14·00m), (62°) 34ft 9$\frac{1}{2}$in (10·60m); length (incl probe) 61ft 6$\frac{1}{4}$in (18·75m); height 15ft 7in (4·75m).
Weights: (-17 estimated, -20 and -22 slightly less) empty 22,046lb (10,000kg); loaded (clean) 30,865lb (14,000kg), (maximum) 41,887lb (19,000kg).
Performance: (-17, clean) maximum speed at sea level 798mph (1284 km/h, Mach 1·05), maximum speed at optimum height 1,432mph (2305 km/h, Mach 2·17); initial climb 45,275ft (13,800m)/min; service ceiling 59,050ft (18,000m); combat radius with 4,410lb (2000kg) external stores (hi-lo-hi) 391 miles (630km).
Armament: Two 30mm NR-30 cannon, each with 70 rounds, in wing roots; eight pylons under fuselage, fixed gloves and swing-wings for maximum external load of 11,023lb (5000kg) including the AS-7 "Kerry" air-to-surface missile (20, -22, six pylons).
History: First public display at Domodedovo 1967; service delivery, possibly 1970 (-17) and 1972–3 (-20).
Users: Egypt (-20), Peru (-22), Poland (-20), Soviet Union (FA, -17).

Development: A logical direct modification of the somewhat limited Su-7B, the Su-17 has variable-geometry "swing-wings" pivoted far outboard, hinged to a slightly modified -7B centre section with strengthened landing gear. At maximum sweep the trailing edge of the centre section aligns with the outer section, and it carries two shallow fences on each side. At the pivots are large square-fronted fences combined with pylons which are stressed to carry 2,200lb (1000kg) stores which in the Polish Su-20 are

Right: Part of a substantial formation of Su-20 variable-geometry attack aircraft in service with the Egyptian Air Force. All versions normally fly with two large jettisonable tanks on the wing-pivot pylons. In the conflict with Libya a few aircraft of this type were in mutual conflict.

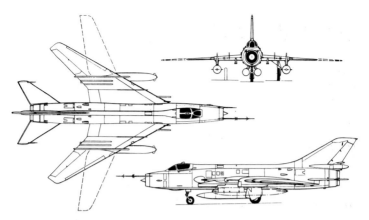

Above: Three-view of Su-20, showing range of wing sweep.

invariably drop tanks with nose fins. The swing-wings carry full-span slats, slotted ailerons and flaps which retract inside the centre section. Compared with the Su-7B the result is the ability to lift twice the external load from airstrips little more than half as long, and climb and level speed at all heights are much increased, even in the lower-powered Su-20 and export Su-22. Equipment in the -17 includes SRD-5M "High Fix" radar, an ASP-5ND fire-control system and comprehensive communications and IFF. Landing performance is so much better than the -7B that a braking chute is not fitted; in its place is the aft-facing aerial for a Sirena 3 radar homing and warning system at the rear of the prominent dorsal spine. Peru's 36 aircraft were to be delivered in 1977.

Left: An Su-20 in service with the PWL (Polish Air Force). Despite various differences this type has the same NATO code of 'Fitter-C' as the Soviet Union's Su-17.

Below: An Su-17 of the Soviet Frontal Aviation based in East Germany. There is a version with extra radar ('Fitter-D').

147

Sukhoi Su-19

Su-19 versions known to NATO as "Fencer"

Origin: The design bureau of Pavel O. Sukhoi, Soviet Union.
Type: Two-seat multi-role combat aircraft.
Engines: Two afterburning turbofan or turbojet engines, probably two 24,500lb (11,113kg) Lyulka AL-21F3.
Dimensions: (Estimated) span (spread, about 22°) 56ft 3in (17·5m), swept (about 72°) 31ft 3in (9·53m); length 69ft 10in (21·29m); height 21ft (6·4m).
Weights: (Estimated) empty 35,000lb (15,875kg); maximum loaded 70,000lb (31,750kg).
Performance: (Estimated) maximum speed, clean, 950mph (1530km/h, Mach 1·25) at sea level, about 1,650mph (2655km/h, Mach 2·5) at altitude; initial climb, over 40,000ft (12,200m)/min; service ceiling, about 60,000ft (18,290m), combat radius with maximum weapons, about 500 miles (805km); ferry range, over 2,500 miles (4025km).
Armament: One 23mm GSh-23 twin-barrel cannon in lower centreline; at least six pylons on fuselage, fixed and swinging wings, for wide range of stores including guided and unguided air-to-ground or air-to-air missiles.
History: First flight, probably about 1970; service delivery, 1974 or earlier.
User: Soviet Union (mainly FA).

Development: First identified publicly in the West by the Chairman of the US Joint Chiefs of Staff, who described the Su-19 as "the first modern Soviet fighter to be developed specifically as a fighter-bomber for the ground-attack mission", this aircraft will probably be the chief tactical attack aircraft of the Soviet V-VS in 1980. Like the rival but much smaller MiG-27, the Su-19 is an extremely clean machine strongly reminiscent of the F-111 and Mirage G, having side-by-side seats and wing and tailplane

Above: This drawing is believed to be as true to life as any yet published — and certainly much better than most, which among other things fail to show a nose large enough to contain the powerful radar. It is worth noting that in 1980, six years after this type entered service and at least 10 years after prototype completion, not one had been seen outside the Soviet Union or even clearly photographed (see below).

Right: In 1980 this blurred shape was still the only authentic illustration of the Su-19 available. It emphasizes the aspect ratio (slenderness in plan shape) of the extremely efficient swingwings, the size of the sensor-studded nose and the large area of the fixed wing gloves, and the main gears which probably have twin wheels.

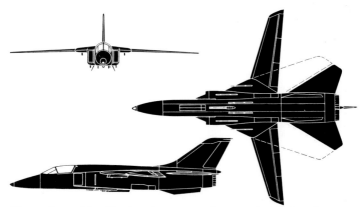

Three-view of Su-19, showing range of sweep (provisional).

at the same level, as in the US machine, yet following the French aircraft in general layout. In general capability the nearest Western equivalent is the F-14 Tomcat, which shows just how formidable this aircraft is. Whereas "Foxbat" was on many Western lips in the 1960s, so is "Fencer" a big scare-word in the 1970s. Features of the first service version include a typical Sukhoi tail, but with ventral fins; double-shock side inlets; full-span slats and double-slotted flaps; and very extensive avionics (thought to include a multi-mode attack radar, doppler, laser ranger and very comprehensive EW/ECM installations).

Tupolev Tu-28P

Tu-28P "Fiddler";
Tupolev bureau, Tu-102 or Tu-128

Origin: The design bureau of Andrei N. Tupolev, Soviet Union.
Type: Long-range all-weather interceptor.
Engines: Originally, two large axial turbojets of unknown type, each with afterburning rating of about 27,000lb (12,250kg), probably similar to those of Tu-22; later versions, afterburning turbofans of about 30,000lb (13,610 kg) each, as in later Tu-22.
Dimensions: (Estimated) span 65ft (20m); length 85ft (26m); height 23ft (7m).
Weights: (Estimated) empty 55,000lb (25,000kg); maximum loaded 100,000lb (45,000kg).
Performance: (Estimated) maximum speed (with missiles, at height) 1,150mph (1850km/h, Mach 1·75); initial climb, 25,000ft (7500m)/min; service ceiling (not gross weight) about 60,000ft (18,000m); range on internal fuel (high Patrol) about 1,800 miles (2900km).
Armament: No guns seen in any version; mix of infra-red homing and radar-homing "Ash" air-to-air guided missiles, originally one of each and since 1965 two of each.
History: First flight, believed 1957; service delivery, probably 1961.
User: Soviet Union (PVO).

Development: Largest fighter known to be in service in the world, this formidable machine is essentially conventional yet has the greatest internal fuel capacity of any fighter and the biggest interception radar known to exist. It was one of a number of supersonic types produced by the Tupolev bureau with technology explored with the family of aircraft of the late 1950s known to NATO as "Backfin" (another is the Tu-22). Like the

Right: A flight-line of what are in many respects the largest interceptors in regular combat service. The Tupolev bureau has played every kind of tune on this classic basic design, relatives of which are seen in the Tu-22 'Blinder' and the swing-wing 'Backfire' long-range multi-role aircraft. It has been reported that the IA-PVO has a missile-armed interceptor version of the Tu-22 in service as a replacement for the Tu-28P.

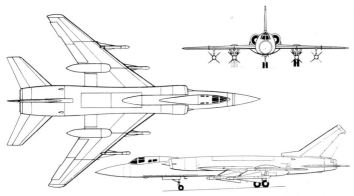

Three-view of the Tu-28P long-range interceptor, with four "Ash" air-to-air missiles.

others the Tu-28P has a distinctive wing with sharply kinked trailing edge, the outer 45° panels being outboard of large fairings extending behind the trailing edge accommodating the four-wheel bogie landing gears. Two crew sit in tandem under upward-hinged canopies, and all armament is carried on wing pylons. Early versions had twin ventral fins and usually large belly fairings, but these features are absent from aircraft in current service. The Tu-28P would be an ideal strategic patrol fighter to operate in conjunction with the "Moss" AWACS.

Left: A typical Tu-28P of the IA-PVO, with NATO code-name of 'Fiddler'. Usually these very large long-range aircraft carry two IR-homing and two radar-homing versions of the 'Ash' air-to-air missile.

Vought A-7 Corsair II

Vought A-7A to K and TA-7C and H

Origin: Vought Systems Division of LTV, Dallas, USA.

Type: Single-seat attack bomber (carrier- or land-based); (TA) dual trainer.

Engine: (A) one 11,350lb (5150kg) thrust Pratt & Whitney TF30-6 two-shaft turbofan; (B, C) 12,200lb (5534kg) TF30-8; (D) 14,250lb (6465kg) Allison TF41-1 (Rolls-Royce Spey derivative) of same layout; (E) 15,000lb (6804kg) TF41-2.

Dimensions: Span 38ft 9in (11·80m); length 46ft 1½in (14·06m); (TA) 48ft 2in (14·68m); height 16ft 0¾in (4·90m); (TA) 16ft 5in (5m).

Weights: Empty (A) 15,904lb (7214kg); (D) 19,781lb (8972kg); maximum loaded (A) 32,500lb (14,750kg); (D) 42,000lb (19,050kg).

Performance: Maximum speed (all single-seat versions, clean) 698mph (1123km/h) at low level; climb and ceiling, not reported (seldom relevant); tactical radius with weapon load, typically 715 miles (1150km); ferry range with four external tanks, typically 4,100 miles (6600km).

Armament: (A, B) two 20mm Colt Mk 12 in nose; six wing and two fuselage pylons for weapon load of 15,000lb (6804kg). (D, E) one 20mm M61 Vulcan cannon on left side of fuselage with 1,000-round drum; external load up to theoretical 20,000lb (9072kg).

History: First flight 27 September 1965; service delivery October 1966; first flight of D, 26 September 1968.

Users: Greece, Pakistan, USA (Air Force, Navy).

Development: Though derived from the Crusader, the Corsair II is a totally ▶

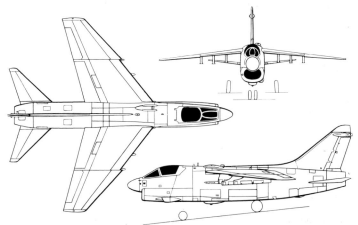

Above: Three-view of Vought A-7D (A-7E generally similar).

Left: An A-7A Corsair II serving during the Vietnam conflict with VA-195 Navy attack squadron embarked aboard USS *Kitty Hawk*. No longer in service.

Below left: A-7Es of the Carrier Air Group embarked aboard USS *America*. The A-7E is the most numerous type in Fleet Attack Squadrons.

Below: An A-7A about to be launched from USS *Constellation* off SE Asia.

different aircraft. By restricting performance to high subsonic speed, structure weight was reduced, range dramatically increased and weapon load multiplied by about 4. Development was outstandingly quick, as was production. Vought built 199 A-7A, used in action in the Gulf of Tonkin on 3 December 1967, followed by 196 B models. The C designation was used for the first 67 E models which retained the TF30 engine. In 1966 the Corsair II was adopted by the US Air Force, the A-7D having the superior TF41 engine, Gatling gun and more complete avionics for blind or automatic weapon delivery under all conditions, with head-up display and inertial/

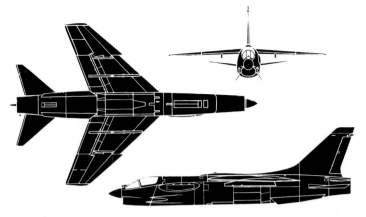

Three-view of F-8J, a remanufactured F-8E now in use with the US Naval Reserve.

Altogether 1,259 were built, plus two prototypes, and in 1966–71 446 were rebuilt to a later standard (B to L, C to K, E to J and D to H). The continual process of improvement added all-weather radar, improved autopilot and weapon-delivery systems, air/ground weapons and, in the 42 F-8E(FN) for the French Navy, slower approach for small carriers. Variants include RF reconnaissance, DF drone RPV and QF RPV-control aircraft; a single dual trainer was also built. Many rebuilt versions remain in combat service, with long life ahead; total Crusader flight time exceeds 3,000,000hr.

Left: An F-8L, one of the long-life remanufactured versions, formerly serving with the USMC (squadron VMF-321).

Below: Rebuilt Crusader, probably an F-8J, serving with VF-201 US Navy fighter squadron. In 1980 French F-8E(FN) fighters were being replaced by the Super Etendard attack aircraft, and the only remaining user is the 7th Tactical Fighter Squadron of the Philippines Air Force.

Yakovlev Yak-36

Yak-36 "Forger A" and -36U (?) "Forger B"

Origin: The design bureau of Aleksander S. Yakovlev, Soviet Union.
Type: Single-seat VTOL naval attack (and possibly reconnaissance) aircraft; ("Forger B") two-seat dual trainer.
Engines: One lift/cruise turbojet or turbofan of unknown type with estimated maximum thrust of 17,000lb (7710kg); two lift jets of unknown type with estimated thrust of 5,600lb (2540kg) each.
Dimensions (estimated): Span 25ft (7·6m); length (A) 49ft 3in (15·0m), (B) 58ft (17·7m); height 13ft 3in (4·0m); width with wings folded 14ft 10in (4·51m).
Weights (estimated): Empty 12,000lb (5450kg) (B slightly heavier); maximum loaded 22,050lb (10,000kg).
Performance (estimated): Maximum speed at sea level 722mph (1160 km/h, Mach 0·95); maximum level speed at optimum height 860mph (1380km/h, Mach 1·3); service ceiling about 50,000ft (15,250m); radius on hi-lo-hi attack mission without external fuel, not greater than 200 miles (320km).
Armament: Contrary to early reports there appears to be no internal gun; four pylons under the non-folding wing centre section carry gun pods, reconnaissance pods, ECM payloads, bombs, missiles (said to include AA-2 "Atoll" AAM and AS-7 "Kerry" ASM) and tanks. Maximum external load, about 4,000lb (1814kg). (B two-seater) none seen.
History: First flight probably about 1971; service delivery possibly 1975.
User: Soviet Union (AV-MF).

Development: At the 1967 show at Domodedovo a single V/STOL jet-lift research aircraft gave a convincing display of hovering and transitions. Called "Freehand" by NATO, it was at first thought to be the Yak-36, but this is now believed to be the service designation of the combat aircraft carried above *Kiev,* the first of the large Soviet carriers (officially classed as anti-submarine cruisers) which also carry ASW helicopters and an unprecedented array of shipboard weapons. The "Freehand", of which fewer than ten are thought to have been built, conducted trials from a specially built platform on the carrier *Moskva'* It provided information to assist the

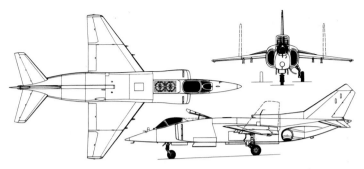

Above: Three-view of single-seat "Forger A" (note wing fold).

design of the Yak-36, which probably has the same large lift turbofan engine plus aft-angled lift jets behind the cockpit. To take off, the three engines must be used together and a vertical ascent made, the main nozzles being rotated to about 100° to balance the rearward thrust of the lift jets. STOL takeoffs are not thought to be possible, neither is Viffing (vectoring in forward flight) to increase combat manoeuvrability. The design is simple, though one wonders why the wing was mounted in the mid-position instead of the much-lighter solution of putting it above the main engine. The latter has plain inlets with a row of auxiliary doors as on the Harrier, but supersonic speed at height is judged possible in the clean condition. Other features include Fowler flaps, large ailerons on the folding outer wings, wingtip and tail control nozzles, a ram inlet duct in the dorsal spine, rear airbrakes, a large vertical tail with dielectric tip, and a dielectric nosecap probably covering a small ranging radar. The "Forger" B has a completely different tandem-seat nose angled downwards and a lengthened rear fuselage to preserve directional stability. The development squadron aboard *Kiev* on her shakedown cruise from the Nikolayev yard to Murmansk flew intensively, and observers especially noted the repeated precision of take-offs and landings, indicating ship guidance. Even this aircraft is almost certainly an interim type.

Below: 'Forger-A' photographed operating from *Kiev* in 1976; some examples of this basic single-seat version lack the row of auxiliary inlet doors between the inlet and painted flag.

Look out for these other
SUPER-VALUE GUIDES!

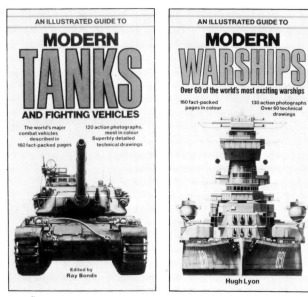

AN ILLUSTRATED GUIDE TO

MODERN
TANKS
AND FIGHTING VEHICLES

The world's major
combat vehicles
described in
160 fact-packed pages

120 action photographs,
most in colour
Superbly detailed
technical drawings

Edited by
Ray Bonds

AN ILLUSTRATED GUIDE TO

MODERN
WARSHIPS

Over 60 of the world's most exciting warships

160 fact-packed
pages in colour

130 action photographs
Over 60 technical
drawings

Hugh Lyon

* Each has 160 fact-filled pages

* Each is colorfully illustrated with action photographs and technical drawings

* Each contains concisely presented data and accurate
  descriptions of major international weapons

* Each represents terrific value

Following soon:
Illustrated guides to

**German, Italian and Japanese
FIGHTERS AND ATTACK AIRCRAFT
of World War II**

**BOMBERS
of World War II**

detailing the exciting combat aircraft that fought in the
most ferocious war in history

.... thousands of facts and figures
.... hundreds of action photos, many in color
.... superb color profiles depicting unit markings
.... highly detailed three-view line drawings

Your military library will be incomplete
without them.

PRINTED IN BELGIUM BY
proost
INTERNATIONAL BOOK PRODUCTION